An Altitud

Rocky Mountain National Park

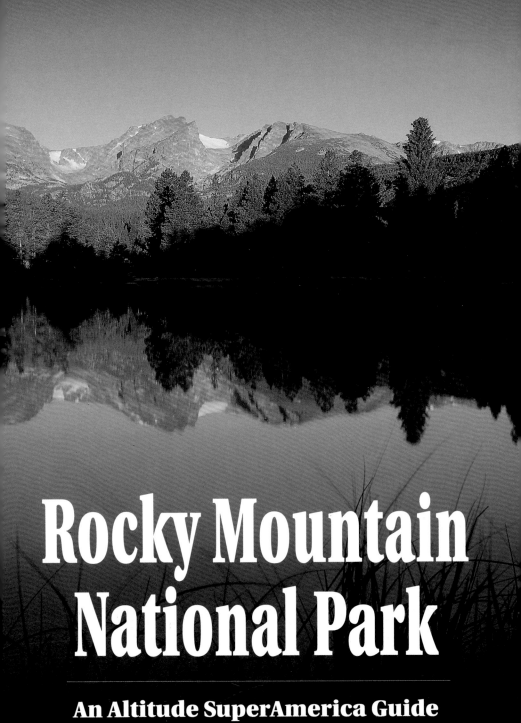

Rocky Mountain
National Park

An Altitude SuperAmerica Guide
by Patrick Soran and Dan Klinglesmith

Publication Information

Altitude Publishing Ltd.
P.O. Box 309, 4255 South Buckley Road
Aurora, CO 80013

Copyright © 1998 Altitude Publishing Ltd.
Text copyright © 1998 Patrick Soran and Dan Klinglesmith

Extreme care has been taken to ensure that all information presented in this book is accurate and up-to-date, and neither the author nor the publisher can be held responsible for any errors.

Cataloging in Publication Data

ISBN 1-55265-001-4

1. Rocky Mountain National Park (Colo.)--Guidebooks.

I. Klinglesmith, Dan 1955–; Soran, Patrick 1953– II. Title.

F782.R59S67 1998   917.88'.690433   C98-910087-1

Front cover photo:
Sprague Lake

Inset front cover:
left: Hikers in Rocky Mountain National Park
right: Rocky Mountain bighorn sheep

Frontispiece:
Reflections in Sprague Lake

Back cover photo:
Longs Peak

Design and Production Team

Concept	Stephen Hutchings
Art direction/design	Stephen Hutchings
Design/layout	Kelly Stauffer
Editor	Sabrina Grobler
Index	Noeline Bridge
Financial management	Laurie Smith

A Note from the Publisher

The world described in *Altitude SuperAmerica Guides* is a unique and fascinating place. It is a world filled with surprise and discovery, beauty and enjoyment, questions and answers. It is a world of people, cities, landscape, animals and wilderness as seen through the eyes of those who live in, work with, and care for this world. The process of describing this world is also a means of defining ourselves.

It is also a world of relationship, where people derive their meaning from a deep and abiding contact with the land–as well as from each other. And it is this sense of relationship that guides all of us at Altitude to ensure that these places continue to survive and evolve in the decades ahead.

Altitude SuperAmerica Guides are books intended to be used, as much as read. Like the world they describe, *Altitude SuperAmerica Guides* are evolving, adapting and growing. Please write to us with your comments and observations, and we will do our best to incorporate your ideas into future editions of these books.

Stephen Hutchings
Publisher

Altitude GreenTree Program
Altitude Publishing will plant twice as many trees as were used in the manufacturing of this product.

Printed and bound in Canada by Friesen Printers

Contents

Maps

The *Rocky Mountain National Park SuperAmerica Guide* is organized according to the following color scheme:

Introduction . . . .

How to Use the Park . . . .

Highlights of Nature . . . .

Rocky Mountain Recreation . . . .

Estes Park . . . .

Vistas and Vales . . . .

The Roof of the Rockies . . . .

Grand Lake . . . .

Reference . . . .

Introduction

Rainbow over The Crags

Welcome to Rocky Mountain National Park—the heart of Colorado's high country. Its 415 square miles straddle the Continental Divide along the dramatic Front Range, a mere hour and a half northwest of Denver. Here, granite peaks—60 rising higher than 12,000 feet above sea level—reach for the brilliant blue sky. Tufted tundra tops the crest of the continent, glacier-gouged valleys splay out like the fingers of a hand cupping nature's montane bounty and splashing streams provide healing waters for threatened species.

This rich habitat—home to four distinct ecosystems—is abundant with the living creatures that have made Colorado famous for its wildlife. Elk call to each other with their plaintive wail; pika, squirrels and yellow-bellied marmots skitter along the rocks; deer gather in aspen groves, their mule-like ears at attention; beavers slap their tails to alert their kin; and raptors drift on crisp, clear air, hundreds of feet above verdant meadows.

Humans occupy the park as well. They come to drive Trail Ridge Road and admire Bear Lake, the park's two most popular attractions. But they also travel here to hike and fish, to spot wildlife, to sniff wildflowers, to clear their heads and reach deep into nature's serenity.

Modern humans aren't the first to cherish this bounty. Ute and Arapaho tribes migrated through these same valleys 150 years ago. Paleo-Indians left arrowheads behind 10,000 years before that. Fur trappers sought beaver pelts along the streams; prospectors scratched the ground for gold.

Rocky Mountain National Park—simply Rocky to its admirers—became a national park in 1915. The nation's tenth national park was established in large part because a man named Enos Mills, a gifted writer and speaker, believed strongly that this area deserved preservation. And he wasn't alone; local ranchers and landowners, such as

left: Longs Peak, Rocky Mountain National Park (cabin removed summer, 1997)

Alexander MacGregor and Abner Sprague, came here to farm this land yet became its stewards, for Rocky is the kind of territory that inspires affection and loyalty.

The park has always been popular. In 1920, it hosted 250,000 visitors; in 1996, more than three million wildlife and wilderness enthusiasts passed through the gates. Although only a fraction the size of Yellowstone or Yosemite National Parks, Rocky greets nearly as many guests. Most people arrive during the summer months and pay a call at the park's two most visited areas.

Trail Ridge Road threads through each of Rocky's four ecosystems. It rises from Deer Ridge Junction, through montane and subalpine forests to drape for miles atop the park's main enticement—its hundred square miles of alpine tundra—before dropping into the rich riparian rewards of the Kawuneeche Valley.

The beauty of Bear Lake reigns from the park's southeastern quadrant. Its setting is one of dazzling splendor, reflecting Hallett Peak and framing views of ice-incised Glacier Basin. Thousands of nature-lovers arrive every day to walk along Bear Lake's shore. Others use it as a staging ground for the lacework of trails weaving together nature's generosity.

Park rangers near the lake coach day-trippers on using the park's resources. Indeed, park personnel have been helping nature-lovers for decades. They have developed shuttle bus systems to alleviate traffic snarls, built visitor centers and museums to educate

Mt. Meeker and Longs Peak

visitors and conducted hundreds of informative talks and demonstrations.

These rangers deal daily with the difficult issues facing Rocky Mountain National Park. Are the abundant elk herds growing too large? Should Rocky's borders be developed? How can threatened and endangered species best be nurtured? Ought wolves and grizzlies be reintroduced?

With its budget shrinking and its user-base expanding, the park's administration recognizes the need to focus on critical priorities. Among these

are balancing wilderness-maintenance principles against the desire of millions of visitors to have an exceptional outdoor experience. Rangers are striving to shepherd park resources wisely in order to ensure that Rocky Mountain National Park thrives for generations to come.

And it doesn't take long to figure out why. A moment spent gazing at a silvery mountain, listening to a bugling elk, sniffing an aromatic sage or caressing the rugged trunk of a Ponderosa pine transforms most park

Rocky Mountain National Park: Just the Facts

Size: 415.2 square miles; 265,727 acres.

Established: January 26, 1915, the nation's 10th oldest park.

Elevations: Park Headquarters Visitor Center: 7,840 feet above sea level; Kawuneeche Visitor Center: 8,720 feet; Trail Ridge Road: 12,183 feet.

Mountains: Highest: Longs Peak, 14,255 feet above sea level, Colorado's 15th highest mountain; 114 named peaks above 10,000 feet; 60 peaks above 12,000 feet; 20 peaks

above 13,000 feet; one above 14,000.

Lakes: 147

Lakes with fish: 50

Bird species: 260

Endangered species present: Peregrine falcon

Populations (as of 1996)
Bighorn sheep: 650
Elk: 2,000 in winter, 3,200 in summer
Mule deer: 250 in winter
Black Bear: 30
Moose and coyote are also common

visitors into park protectors. Many people arrive as observers and depart feeling like caretakers of this precious place.

How to Use This Book

This is a handbook to Rocky Mountain National Park. It explains the lay of the land, reveals the park's highlights and explores its cultural and natural histories. It gives tips on bypassing the crowds and how to make great photographs and videos, as well as suggesting itineraries. It tells readers where to find wildlife and how to respect habitats. It illustrates the four ecosystems that are found in Rocky. It provides information about the animals visitors are most likely to see. Plus, it introduces readers to several people to whom Rocky Mountain National Park has been entrusted—its rangers.

Chapter two—"How to Use the Park"—includes the practical information so essential to charting a successful stay: How to get there? What to wear? What's the weather going to be like? Where is gasoline available? How does the shuttle system work? How much are the fees? Is it safe to eat the snow? Should bears be a concern? What about altitude sickness? "Using the Park" responds to these questions.

"High-

lights of Nature," the book's third chapter, explores Rocky's setting in the natural world. Outlining geology, climate and ecosystems, it also takes an in-depth look at how glaciers sculpted much of the park's terrain. Twelve pages illustrate the park's most visible plants and animals.

The book's next chapter—"Rocky Mountain Recreation"—is devoted to Rocky Mountain National Park's outdoor activities. It explains how to choose the perfect hike and suggests a kit of first-aid equipment. In addition to hiking, many other recreational topics are covered, including camping, backcountry use, horseback riding, bicycling, fishing, rafting, swimming, skiing, snowshoeing and snowmobiling.

Two chapters—five and eight—dedicate themselves to Estes Park and Grand Lake; Rocky's eastern and western gateway cities. These hamlets provide accommodations, meals and amusement for park visitors. Layout, history and attractions accompany information about what to do with children, where to camp and upcoming festivals.

But the heart of this

book lies in chapters six and seven. Echoing the way most visitors use the park, these sections divide Rocky into its high-altitude drives and its lower-elevation parklands.

Chapter six, "Vistas and Vales," explores the valleys—playgrounds, really—that rest at the base of Rocky Mountain National Park's massive peaks. This chapter provides hike recommendations, museum descriptions and pointers on where to find autumn's most spectacular color.

The next chapter is titled "The Roof of the Rockies," for it comments on every pull-out along the park's two top-of-the-world byways: Trail Ridge Road (a macadam two-lane that's the highest continuously paved road in the United States); and the Old Fall River Road (a gravel one-way that ascends through a dozen switchbacks into alpine tundra). A reference section rounds out the guide. It's complete with dozens of hotel and restaurant listings, tourism information contacts, and federal, regional and local information sources.

following pages: Tundra Granites, & the Never Summer Mountains

Rocky Mountain bighorn sheep

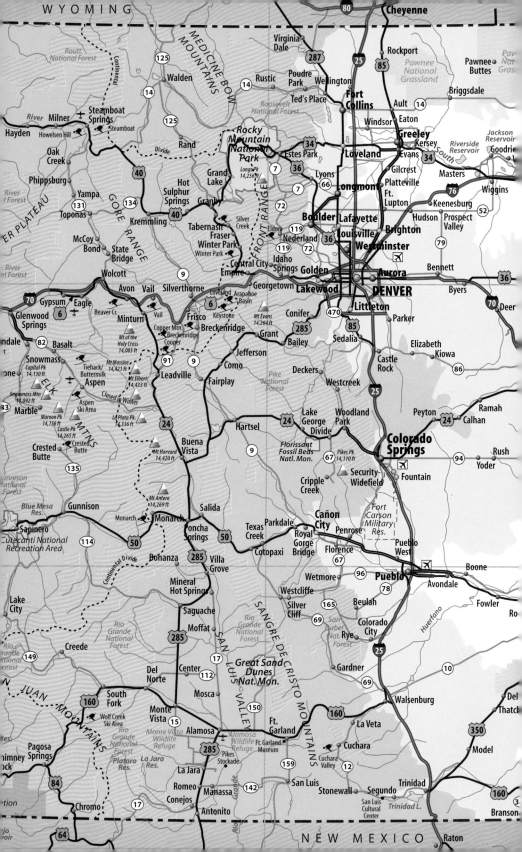

How to Use the Park

Guided hike in Moraine Park

Rocky Mountain National Park is one of the easiest-to-use parks in the national park system. It's a breeze to get to, simple to find your way around in and its eastern and western gateway cities offer splendid activities, accommodations and restaurants. Yet the park can seem a

little intimidating: What are the rules? Where are the information sources? Are pets allowed? What is there for kids to do?

A stay in Rocky, whether it be for a week or a day, goes more smoothly with a little practical information at hand.

Getting to Rocky Mountain National Park

Via Estes Park
The eastern gateway to Rocky Mountain National Park, it lies 65 miles northwest of Denver. **Fastest route:** Take U.S. Inter-state 25 north out of Denver to U.S. Highway 36 to Boulder. Follow U.S. 36 through Boulder and Lyons to Estes Park; travel time—about 1.5 hours. **Most scenic route:** In Boulder, turn onto Canyon Boulevard, (U.S. 7/Colorado 119). Stay on the spectacular Colorado Highway 119 to Nederland, then turn north onto Colorado Highway 72 and stay on this vista-laden road to Raymond. Head north (left) on Colorado Highway 7 into Estes Park. Not nearly as complicated as it sounds, this route from Nederland north is the Peak to Peak

Scenic and Historic Byway— by far the most panoramic way to the park. **Historic route:** U. S. Interstate 25 north out of Denver to U. S. Highway 34 west (toward Loveland). This is the longest route but follows the Big Thompson River through "The Narrows"—the cliff-sided raceway of the 1976 flood that killed 145 people. You can still see the high-water mark in places.

Via Grand Lake
The west gateway to Rocky is easily reached via U.S. Highways 40 and 34 north off U. S.

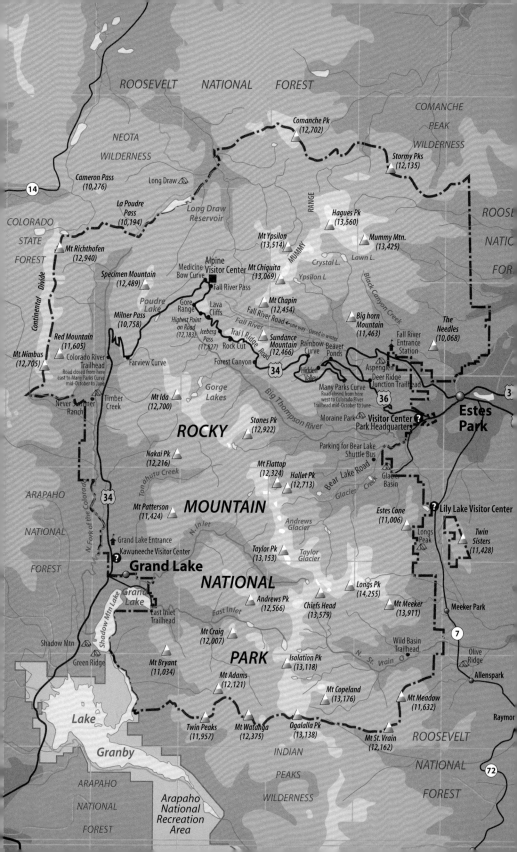

Interstate 70 west of Idaho Springs. This route takes visitors over scenic Berthoud Pass and past the Winter Park and Silver Creek ski areas.

Park Visitor Centers

Visitor centers are also discussed in later chapters.

Park Headquarters: The headquarters is open daily except Christmas at its location three miles west of Estes Park on U.S. Highway 36. The headquarters has an auditorium, book store, displays and administrative offices. For hours of operation call 970-586-1206.

Moraine Park Museum: The park's finest museum is located in a renovated lodge at the east end of Moraine Park. Reach it by driving one-and-a-half miles beyond the Beaver Meadows Entrance and turning south onto Bear Lake Road. Behind the museum, a self-guided trail explains many features of the park's natural history. Open daily from early May through September.

Alpine Visitor Center: Located well above treeline in the alpine tundra ecosystem, the Alpine Visitor Center is 20 miles west of Beaver Meadows Entrance on Trail Ridge Road. It has the only food facility inside the park as well as the only gift shop. Open daily from Memorial Day through Columbus Day.

Lily Lake Visitor Center: On Colorado Highway 7 (also called the Peak to Peak Scenic and Historic Byway), Lily Lake has easy-to-read displays that provide information on both Rocky Mountain National Park and the surrounding national forests. Open June through September.

Kawuneeche Visitor Center: The only center on the west side of the park, Kawuneeche guides visitors to the park's lesser-known western flank. Open year round (except Christmas); alongside U.S. Highway 34 near Grand Lake.

When to Visit Rocky

Spring is the wettest time in Rocky; chances of rain or wet spring snow are high. Yet as the deep snow pack melts, impromptu waterfalls form, wildlife is on the move and wildflowers sprout at the lower elevations, even while snow covers the higher slopes. High temperatures run from 40° to 60° Fahrenheit during April and 45° to 70° in May. Trail Ridge Road generally opens in late May and Old Fall River Road opens around July 4th.

Summer brings nearly perfect weather. In June, expect many clear days with daytime temperatures between 55° and 80°. July is perhaps the finest summer month to visit Rocky Mountain National Park. Although many sites may be crowded at this time, the weather is almost always sunny (in the morning at least), the wildflowers are at their peak at both the low and high elevations and elk and bighorn sheep tend to make daily appearances. Throughout the summer, evenings can be chilly. August, while still spectacular, brings many rainy afternoons and fewer flowers.

Visitors who seek great swaths of gold, abundant wildlife and smaller crowds come in autumn. Snow can arrive in September, often followed by every Coloradan's favorite mini-season: Indian Summer—warm, fragrant days and cool, crisp nights. The aspen usually pull on their multi-colored shawls in September. The elk come down from the high country for their mating—with its attendant "bulging"—in mid- to late September. Hiking trails are not crowded at this time. In October, things can get downright cold: daytime temperatures range from 30° to 60° in the day.

Winter brings abundant snow—up to 300 inches in some areas. Cross-country skiing is excellent, and the park is beautifully draped in white. Roads to Bear Lake and Cub Lake trailhead, as well as Trail Ridge Road as far as Many

---

SuperAmerica Guide Recommends: Ten Best Views

In 415 square miles, great vistas are sure to reveal themselves. Here are ten of the best.
- Longs Peak from the Moraine Park Museum.
- Hallett Peak from Nymph Lake.
- Glacier Basin from Bear Lake.
- Mountains, parks and plains from Many Parks Curve.
- Longs Peak from MacGregor Ranch.
- The Kawuneeche Valley from Farview Curve.
- The Big Thompson River Valley from Forest Canyon Overlook.
- Estes Park from atop the aerial tram.
- Grand Lake from the porch of the Grand Lake Lodge.
- The Grand Lake area from the fire tower on Shadow Mountain (hike required).

---

left: Rocky Mountain National Park

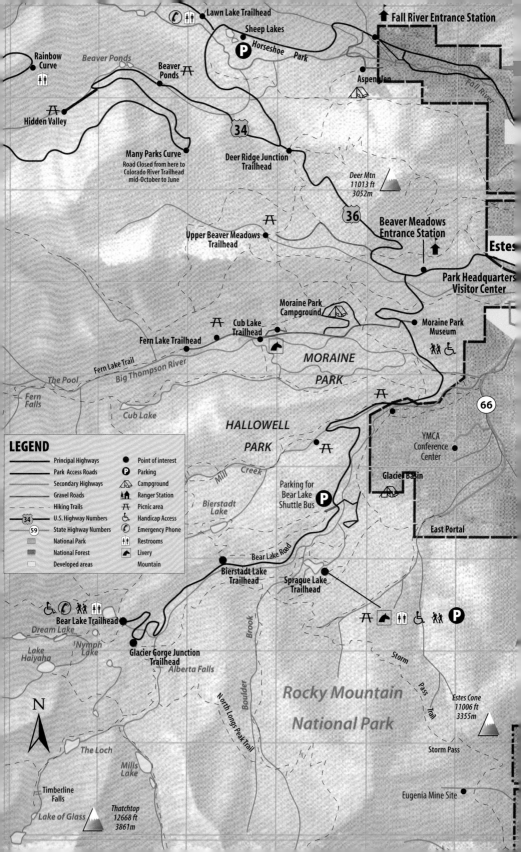

Fall River Entrance Station

Lawn Lake Trailhead

Sheep Lakes

Horseshoe Park

P

Rainbow Curve

Beaver Ponds

Beaver Ponds

Aspenglen

Hidden Valley

34

Many Parks Curve
Road Closed from here to
Colorado River Trailhead
mid-October to June

Deer Ridge Junction Trailhead

Deer Mtn
11013 ft
3052m

36

Beaver Meadows Entrance Station

Estes

Upper Beaver Meadows Trailhead

Park Headquarters Visitor Center

Moraine Park Campground

Moraine Park Museum

MORAINE PARK

Fern Lake Trailhead

Cub Lake Trailhead

Fern Lake Trail

Big Thompson River

The Pool

Fern Falls

Cub Lake

66

HALLOWELL PARK

YMCA Conference Center

Mill Creek

Glacier Basin

LEGEND

—	Principal Highways	●	Point of interest
—	Park Access Roads	Ⓟ	Parking
—	Secondary Highways	⛺	Campground
—	Gravel Roads	🏠	Ranger Station
---	Hiking Trails	🧺	Picnic area
34	U.S. Highway Numbers	♿	Handicap Access
59	State Highway Numbers	☎	Emergency Phone
	National Park	🚻	Restrooms
	National Forest	🛶	Livery
	Developed areas	⛰	Mountain

Parking for Bear Lake Shuttle Bus

P

East Portal

Bierstadt Lake

Bear Lake Road

Bierstadt Lake Trailhead

Sprague Lake Trailhead

P

Storm Pass Trail

Bear Lake Trailhead

Dream Lake

Nymph Lake

Glacier Gorge Junction Trailhead

Lake Haiyaha

Alberta Falls

North Longs Peak Trail

Boulder Brook

Rocky Mountain

National Park

Estes Cone
11006 ft
3355m

N

The Loch

Mills Lake

Storm Pass

Timberline Falls

Eugenia Mine Site

Lake of Glass

Thatchtop
12668 ft
3861m

Parks Curve, are kept cleared.

Shuttle System

During the busy summer months, automobile traffic can be quite heavy, particularly in the Bear Lake area. Shuttle buses run daily from the Glacier Basin shuttle bus parking area to Bear Lake every 10 to 20 minutes. The busses stop at several trailheads along the way.

In addition, a bus alternates between the Fern Lake trailhead and the shuttle bus parking area approximately once an hour, with stops at Moraine Park Museum and both the Moraine Park and Glacier Basin Campgrounds.

Dressing for Rocky

Think layers throughout the summer, fall, winter and spring. In the summer, the most popular time for a visit, mornings and evenings are usually cool while the mid-day heat can feel debilitating. Dressing in layers allows park visitors to warm up or cool down as needed.

Rain gear is a good idea in spring and summer: afternoon rain showers are common.

Shoes are particularly important during a hike. They should fit well to avoid blisters and to provide better traction. Tennis or running shoes are usually sufficient for easy hikes, but any arduous hiking or climbing should be undertaken only with proper foot gear.

Park Fees

Park fees have increased over recent years as the park service's budget has decreased. The fee for one to seven days for a single vehicle is $10. For a hiker or cyclist, the fee is $6. An annual pass to Rocky Mountain National Park is $20. A Golden Eagle Passport, good for 12 months at any U.S. national park is $50. A Golden Age Passport is $20 for U.S. citizens or permanent residents. The park is free to persons with disabilities.

Road Information

Trail Ridge Road—the park's centerpiece—is typically open from Memorial Day until the first heavy snow of autumn,

---

How to Take Great Pictures

Rocky Mountain National Park is full of great photographic opportunities. Here are some tips for taking home professional-quality photographs.

• Morning and evening light is the most dramatic.

• Make sure the sun is behind you. The light should be falling on the subject of the photo.

• Use a zoom lens to fill up the picture with the subject.

• Carry your camera to be prepared when a great photo opportunity presents itself.

• Shoot wide subjects horizontally, but don't be afraid to turn the camera to vertical.

• Compose the photograph so the subject—be it a child's head or an elk—is slightly off center, facing towards the larger part of the picture.

• Don't take every picture from eye-level. Get down close to the wildflowers or stand up on a rock to get a view from above a lake.

• Take pictures of people doing things: hiking, eating, playing cards. People will appear more relaxed and natural than if they are posing.

Making Great Videos

Shooting videos full of the excitement and beauty of the park is easy.

• Make sure your camera has batteries and that you're up to speed on how the camera works.

• Try different types of shots: Long shots, taking in a large area; medium, which aims at a specific subject; and close-up, which pulls you right into the subject.

• Choose someone to narrate the film. They can step in front of the camera and explain where you are and what you're seeing.

• Short shots are more interesting than ones that go on for several minutes.

• Avoid the temptation to move the camera often; let the subject do the moving.

• Ask yourself before each shot, "Is this really interesting?"

• Try stopping the camera before zooming. The pros use this a lot: shoot, stop, zoom in or out and then start filming again.

• Use a tripod or some other support on long, tight shots. This makes for less wobble.

• Make sure the camera is focused on the subject that you (not the camera) have chosen.

• Look for dramatic lighting, action and individual people.

---

left: Rocky Mountain National Park near the town of Estes Park

which usually occurs in October or November. Trail Ridge is kept plowed during the winter from the east entrance to as high as Many Parks Curve, and on the west entrance from Grand Lake to the Milner Pass/Continental Divide pull-off. Bear Lake Road is kept clear all the way to the lake.

Old Fall River Road—open only during summer—is a one-way, gravel road that climbs from Horseshoe Park to the Alpine Visitor Center. This road has tight switchbacks and is not recommended for recreational vehicles. Trailers and vehicles over 25 feet in length are not allowed. Old Fall River Road offers stunning vistas of the Mummy Range and provides a real sense of being surrounded first by Ponderosa parkland, subalpine forest and finally, by alpine tundra.

U.S. Highway 34, which passes by Sheep Lakes, sometimes closes for five or ten minutes during the spring and summer because bighorn sheep come down to the lake to lick the mineral-rich mud.

Park Newsletter

An excellent source of information, *High Country Headlines*, is handed out at entrance stations, visitor centers and ranger stations. It contains advice about using the park and publishes a schedule of seasonal and ranger-led activities and events.

Services

Services involving cars, banks, groceries, health and laundry facilities are located in Estes Park and Grand Lake.

Food and Lodging

A cafe is located in the Trail Ridge Store adjacent to the Alpine Visitor Center. Otherwise, all food and lodging are located in Estes Park and Grand Lake.

Gift Shops

The only gift shop in Rocky is in the Trail Ridge Store next to the Alpine Visitor Center.

Book Shops

Books, calendars, postcards, tapes and films are offered in the book centers in each of the visitor centers as well as in the Moraine Park Museum.

Lost and Found

Call 970-586-1242 to track down any lost or report any found items.

Post Offices

Post offices are located in Estes Park and Grand Lake.

Stores and Supplies

Only ice and firewood are available for sale in the campgrounds. For food and other supplies, head to Grand Lake or Estes Park.

Handicap Services

All visitor centers are handicap accessible, providing parking spaces and ramps where needed. Fully accessible restrooms are located at Moraine Park Museum, Kawuneeche Visitor Center, Park Headquarters and the Alpine Visitor Center. Facilities at Bear Lake are also wheelchair accessible, as are some of the campgrounds.

Visitor centers also provide trail guides and literature about the park in Braille and on cassette. Some information is available in large-print format.

Call 970-586-1319 for a Telecommunications Device for the Deaf (TDD).

Sprague Lake offers a number of accessible opportunities. The half-mile-long nature trail is flat and smooth. The

Where to Find Wildlife

Rocky is alive with many different types of wildlife: eagles, marmots, squirrels, elk, bighorn sheep, coyote and deer, to name just a few. For the most successful wildlife spotting be patient, have binoculars at the ready and go searching in the early morning or late afternoon.

Deer: These mid-sized mammals are plentiful around dusk between the Beaver Meadows Entrance Station and the Moraine Park Museum.

Elk: In the summer months, look for small, brown dots on the alpine tundra off Trail Ridge Road. In autumn, look for them in the lower valleys such as at Beaver Meadows and near Sheep Lakes.

Bighorn Sheep: The craggy ridges from near Fall River Entrance Station as far as Sheep Lakes support many sheep. Look for gray shapes that don't quite fit in. Sheep often make appearances in the neighborhood of Sheep Lake, especially in spring and summer. Also, visit Sheep Rock west of the Milner Pass turnout.

Small mammals: Almost any walk along any trail will rouse some squirrels. Look for yellow-bellied marmots above timberline and tiny pikas in the rock piles.

Moose: Look for brown masses amid the willows along the Colorado River in the Kawuneeche Valley.

Sprague Lake Handicamp is a group camp, available by reservation only, which is laid out to welcome guests with disabilities. Call 970-586-1242 to gather information.

The trail around Lily Lake, across Colorado Highway 7 from the Lily Lake Visitor Center, is level and accessible. Coyote Valley Trail, on the west side of the park, is an accessible route following a stretch of the Colorado River. Beginning five miles north of the west entrance, the trail has interpretive signs explaining natural and cultural phenomena.

Classes and Seminars

Classes, lectures and guided hikes are offered almost daily. Ask a ranger, inquire at a visitor center or pick up a copy of *High Country Headlines*. In addition, the Rocky Mountain Nature Association offers dozens of seminars that focus on a wide range of topics. Classes include such things as aquatic ecosystems, painting the Rockies, elk studies, mountain ecology, macro-photography and wildflower studies. For information, call the seminar coordinator at 970-586-0108.

Fires

Human-caused fires pose a major threat to Rocky Mountain National Park. Build fires only in designated pits and bury every fire with dirt.

Theft

Do not leave valuables unattended in your car or camp. If a theft occurs, notify a ranger.

Vapor Lock

Cars adjusted to lower altitudes often experience vapor lock at the higher elevations of the park. In such cases, cars have trouble starting, the engine runs less smoothly and there is a loss of engine power. One of the best preventatives is to refrain from running the air conditioning. Another is to stay in a lower gear while climbing.

At the first sign of stalling, shift into neutral and give the engine some gas. If the car does stall, coast to a safe spot on the road and let the engine cool. Don't try to start it repeatedly or it will flood and the battery will wear down. When starting, put the pedal to the floor—don't pump it.

Safety Concerns

Emergency Numbers

For emergencies or help in the park, call either park headquarters at 970-586-1399 or dial 911.

Emergency Telephone Locations

Bear Lake Parking Lot
Cow Creek Trailhead
Lawn Lake Trailhead
Longs Peak Ranger Station
Wild Basin Ranger Station

Kids in the Park

Kids get special enjoyment out of Rocky Mountain National Park.
- The park's specially designed program for children is called "Rocky's Junior Rangers." Visitor centers provide books that list a variety of things to do. After children complete the activities, they hand the book back to a ranger to receive a badge. Activities focus on wildlife, natural preservation and safety.
- The Rocky Mountain Nature Association hosts an art program designed for children to participate in guided art activities. A small fee is charged and a sketchbook is required.
- During a ranger-led "Junior Ranger Adventure" children ages six to ten learn about how nature works and how humans affect it. Check *High Country Headlines* for days and times.
- Rangers perform wildlife-oriented puppet shows at Moraine Park Museum twice a week. See the *High Country Headlines* for days and times.
- The west side of the park has several programs oriented toward children aged six to twelve years old: "Come Bug a Ranger" brings up fun facts about bugs; "Feathers and Such" tickles those who fancy birds; "The Fire Ranger" features red-hot information about fires; "Wilderness Clues" ferrets out what to look for to spot wild animals. Children must be accompanied by an adult.
- "Rocky After Dark" is a ranger program for kids and adults that explores the activities that darkness brings; many animals only come out at night. Kids also learn to identify things by touch alone. Bring a jacket and a flashlight.
- A horseback ride is a good way, particularly for older children, to get a different view of the park and spend some time in the wild.

Lightning

Lightning is a frequent—and dangerous—occurrence. Storms move across the park almost every summer afternoon. Stay off ridges and peaks and avoid lone objects such as large rocks and trees. Move to lower elevations if a storm threatens. If you get caught in a storm, crouch low with your hands around your knees.

Lost Children

The park can be a dangerous and frightening place for a lost child. Children should stay with the group when hiking. If the child is old enough to understand, provide a whistle with instructions to use it only in case of an emergency. Teach kids to stay put if they get lost, as this makes it easier to find them.

Animal Alert

Be alert for animals crossing roadways. Excercise particular caution at dawn and twilight, as animals are most active during these times.

Snow and Ice Fields

Even in summer, these fields of snow or ice can be dangerous. Do not attempt to traverse a snowfield unless you are equipped and experienced. Avoid sliding on the snow; it is easy to lose control and have a serious fall onto the jagged rocks usually found at the bottom of these fields.

The reddish-colored snow on snowfields—called watermelon snow—may contain *giardia lamblia,* which can cause diarrhea and other health problems.

Bears

Bears can be dangerous if provoked while feeding or protecting their cubs. Making plenty of noise during a hike will often scare bears off. Never feed bears (or any other animal in the park). If you encounter a bear on a hike, talk gently to it and back off. Do not turn and run or climb a tree.

Clean your picnic or campsite before you leave. During overnight stays, supplies must be suspended 10 feet above the ground in a tree and four feet away from the trunk.

Swimming

While those tranquil lakes look beautiful, they are actually quite cold. Streams, too, look refreshing but their currents can be deceptively dangerous. Swimming in streams or lakes is not recommended.

Health Concerns

Giardia

Although the waters of the park look harmless, many lakes and streams contain a microscopic organism called *Giardia lamblia.* Within a few days of ingestion, these parasites may cause diarrhea, bloating, cramps and weight loss. A doctor's treatment is required. Any water should be boiled for five to ten minutes prior to drinking to prevent a *giardia* infection.

Altitude Troubles

Oxygen concentrations in the park at high elevations are only about half that of the air at sea level. Even fit climbers often notice the effects of the altitude. Symptoms of altitude sickness include shortness of breath, headache, tiredness, nasal congestion, dizziness and nausea. While these may cause mild discomfort for some, they can be quite serious for others. If symptoms persist or worsen, go to a lower altitude and see a physician.

The best way to avoid altitude sickness is to acclimatize gradually. Stay a day or two in Estes Park or Grand Lake before you head across Trail Ridge Road.

The park also advises limiting strenuous activity; rest, eat lightly, avoid alcohol and increase your fluid intake. If you crave a nap, take one.

Hypothermia

The windy, wet and cold weather that is often prevalent at high altitudes can cause the body's temperature to drop to unsafe levels. Symptoms of hypothermia include shivering and disorientation. Always carry layers of clothing and rain gear when hiking. A hat and gloves are recommended as well. If you show the warning signs, get to a warm place as soon as possible, bundle up and drink warm, non-alcoholic liquids.

Sun Exposure

The ultraviolet rays of the sun burn with particular intensity at higher elevations. Protect skin with long pants and long-sleeved shirts. Wear plenty of sunscreen. Shade your eyes with sunglasses.

Dehydration

The low humidity of the high country, sometimes coupled with strong winds, can cause dehydration. Drink plenty of fluids, even if you are not thirsty. Always carry water on hikes.

Ticks

Ticks are cold-blooded parasites that thrive in brush, grass and woody areas from

Longs Peak

February until mid-July. They feed on the blood of birds and mammals, including humans. To prevent a bite, which may contain infection, tuck trouser cuffs into socks, inspect your clothes, scalp and skin often during hikes as well as after, and use a tick repellent.

If you find a tick on your skin, pull it straight out using tweezers. Remove the body and the entire head.

Two serious illnesses are carried by ticks. Symptoms such as head and body aches, lethargy, nausea and vomiting, abdominal pain, sensitivity to light and a skin rash may indicate Colorado Tick Fever. Conversely, fever, a spotted rash starting on ankles and wrists then spreading, headache, nausea, vomiting and aching muscles and abdomen may indicate Rocky Mountain Spotted Fever. Both should be treated by a doctor, who should be advised that you may have been bitten by a tick.

Lyme disease is common among white-tailed deer in the northeast states. It is very rare in Colorado; no case has ever been reported in Estes Park or Larimer County.

Park Regulations

Pets

Pets are not allowed on any of the hiking or nature trails, or in the backcountry. Certified guide dogs are allowed on trails and in buildings. Pets are allowed, however, in established campgrounds, picnic areas, on roadways and in parking lots. They must be on a leash with a maximum six-foot length, or in a cage. Owners must accompany their pets at all times.

Camping

Camping is allowed only in areas designated as campgrounds. Backcountry camping requires a special permit.

Vehicles

All vehicles must remain on roadways or in parking lots. No off-road driving is allowed. Pull over and park only in designated areas. Seatbelt and child restraint laws apply.

Wildlife

Do not feed or attempt to touch any living creature. Feeding rodents (squirrels) or birds only increases their populations to unhealthy levels. Do not chase the wildlife. No hunting or harassing of wildlife is permitted.

Plant Life

Do not pick wildflowers. Staying on trails protects the flora for others to enjoy. Regulations prohibit the disturbance or removal of public property.

Bicycles

Bicycles are allowed only on designated roadways. Trail riding or backcountry riding is not allowed.

Alcoholic Beverages

Open containers of alcohol are not allowed in cars while on the road or in parking lots. All driving-under-the-influence laws apply.

Got a Question?

Need some Info?
The telephone number for Rocky Mountain National Park is 970-586-1206

Jeff Maugans, Park Ranger

Hired as a "seasonal" ranger with the National Park Service nearly 20 years ago, Jeff Maugans has been an interpretive ranger at Rocky since 1990. He was born and raised in eastern Pennsylvania.

Jeff Maugans

What kind of guidance would you give a young person interested in becoming a park ranger?
Fostering an interest is the biggest step; visit local, state and national parks to develop a deep love for the outdoors. You have to love something to be in a frame of mind to fight for its preservation and protection. In the Park Service, we believe we are an important piece of the environmental community.

Next comes reading and school. Kids should read as much about natural and cultural history as they can as well as doing projects that provide opportunities to focus on nature. Get an education that will confer a strong degree in their field of interest.

Finally, people coming into the service need to be flexible and patient. It can be hard to get a full-time job, so most people start seasonally. Plus, they need to be willing to move around a bit. I worked at six parks before I got to Rocky.

How did you get started?
I always knew I wanted to work out-of-doors. Luckily, the college I went to, Pennsylvania State University, had a program in Environmental Education and Interpretive Services. I started as a seasonal ranger at Mammoth Caves National Park in Kentucky. My

first permanent job was at Edison National Historic Site in New Jersey.

How did you end up at Rocky?
I was lucky because Rocky is a park a lot of people want to work in. I was in the right place at the right time.

What's the typical day for a ranger?
There really is no such thing; every day brings different activities. Some days are spent helping at visitor centers or museums. Many days are spent out in the field leading walks and talks.

How do the ranger-led programs work?
It depends on the topic. For most programs, we focus on the general ecology of an area. We try to interpret the resource that happens to be there. Bird walks and astronomy are my specialties.

What do you mean by "interpret?"
Some people think it means that we're talking a foreign language. It's not foreign but it is the language of the resource. We teach about the geology, history, habitats, plants and animals. And we

try to weave in important issues.

What are some of the issues facing Rocky?
The question of the elk is a big one. Are there too many? Are they harming the park because they eat so much? We're finishing a five-year study now that should give us some answers.

Non-native plant species are a problem too. Things such as non-native thistle and Leafy spurge are choking out other important plants.

What do rangers do in the winter?
Many "seasonals" travel to another park. Some seasonal rangers here go to Everglades or Death Valley National Parks. That way, they end up working pretty much year-round and broadening their experience.

Permanent rangers like myself get ready for the next year. We decide which programs work and which don't and develop new ones. We work on exhibits and do some writing—even take vacations.

Could you talk about the biggest benefit to being a ranger?
We get to make a difference. Rangers are among the big players in the environmental camp and we get to spread the word about protecting our resources. We want visitors to go home feeling like they are stewards not just of the park, but of all cultural and natural resources.

Ranger Programs

One of the most enjoyable things about a visit to any national park is to meet the park rangers, whose job it is to protect the park's resources. And one of the best ways to meet a ranger and to learn something about the park itself is to attend a ranger-led park program.

These popular programs look at a variety of topics such as mammals, plants, geology or birds. They use lectures, walks or discussions that run from one-half to four hours to teach these topics. Some take place every day, while others occur only once or twice a week. All require that children be accompanied by an adult.

The following list describes only the programs that occur most frequently; many other programs are offered each day. For up-to-the minute information, check *High Country Headlines*, which is handed out upon entry into the park.

EAST SIDE PROGRAMS

Hiking at Rocky—This daily program discusses places to go and things to see in the park. Park Headquarters; half an hour; daily.

Moraine Park Nature Walk—Unravel mysteries and sharpen your senses as the Moraine Park landscape is explored. Moraine Park Museum; one hour; daily.

Pathways to Peaks—Discover past efforts and current challenges of building and plowing high-country roads in Arctic-like conditions. Alpine Visitor Center; half an hour; daily.

Rocky After Dark—Sense the

Park ranger

wilderness come alive as darkness settles over the mountains. Bring a flashlight and warm clothes. Limited to 35 participants, each person must be present to make a reservation the day of the program. Reservations must be made at Moraine Park Museum. Moraine Park Museum; 1.5 hours; daily.

Flood of '82—Discover the incredible force of water that changed the landscape in the area of the alluvial fan. Alluvial Fan west parking lot; 1.5 hours; six days per week.

Rivers of Ice—Learn how glaciers shaped the spectacular landscape of Rocky Mountain National Park. Moraine Park Museum; half an hour; daily.

Tracking a Glacier—See and feel the tracks of the glacier that formed Moraine Park. Cub Lake Trailhead; 1.5 hours; five times per week.

Rocky's Engineers—Learn about beaver adaptations and how this large rodent alters Rocky's environment. Hollowell Park; 1.5 hours; six days per week.

Sheep Encounters—The natural history of Rocky's bighorn sheep is revealed in this talk. Sheep Lakes Information Kiosk;

half an hour; twice daily.

Tundra Nature Walk—Exhilarate your senses with sweeping alpine views and miniature wildflower gardens unique to this land above the trees. Dress warmly and bring wind gear. Alpine Visitor Center; 1.5 hours; daily.

Elk Echos—Autumn program about elk adaptations, migration and mating. Moraine Park Campground Amphitheater and West Horseshoe Park parking areas; half an hour; nightly.

All-day Ecology Hike—Join a ranger for a moderately strenuous six to seven mile round-trip hike to a subalpine lake. Learn more about the park's geology, wildlife, subalpine forests and general ecology. Park Headquarters; fee charged; six to seven hours; five times per week.

Campground Programs—Evening programs are held nightly in Aspenglen, Glacier Basin and Moraine Park campgrounds as well as at the Park Headquarters.

WEST SIDE PROGRAMS

Skins and Things—Examine the skins, skulls, antlers and bones of many park mammals. Kawuneeche Visitor Center; one hour; daily.

Historic Never Summer Ranch—Interpretive tours and self-guided half-mile walks. Never Summer Ranch; length varies; daily.

Timber Creek Campfire Program—Nightly slide presentation. Timber Creek Campground; one hour; nightly.

23

A Message from the Rangers...

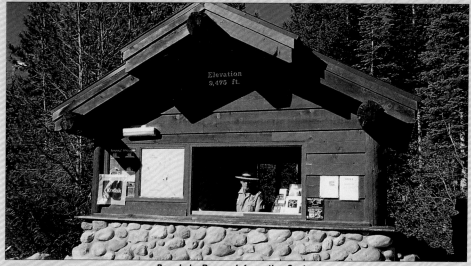

Bear Lake Ranger Information Center

At its inception in the late 19th century, the national park idea was an innovative and startling concept. In fact, the parks are considered by some observers to be America's finest contribution to world culture. However, the national parks find themselves at the doorstep of the second millenium with their future clouded by increasing visitation and the resultant impacts on both natural and manmade resources. The development of neighboring private lands, the vagaries of shifting political philosophies and policies plus continuing federal budgetary constraints are also important considerations.

Rocky Mountain National Park, the nation's tenth oldest, was established in 1915 by Congress with a dual—and somewhat contradictory—purpose: "with regulations being primarily aimed at the freest use of the park for recreation purposes by the public and for the preservation of the natural conditions and scenic

beauties thereof." During ensuing years, a large body of laws and regulations evolved to provide the National Park Service with the necessary authorities to fulfill this double mission.

Up through World War II, accomplishing this task was simpler for park managers than it is today. Although the boundaries of Rocky Mountain National Park represented political boundaries rather than complete ecosystems, Park Service employees had the luxury of concentrating on what took place inside the park itself, because little was going on outside. The United States west of the Mississippi was still a land of open spaces.

But all this has changed. From Colorado's Front Range to Jackson, Wyoming, and the Greater Yellowstone area; from communities around Glacier National Park to cities such as Las Vegas, Phoenix, Albuquerque and Salt Lake City; once wide- open lands are now sites for tract housing,

vacation homes, golf courses, resorts and businesses. Now the parks can no longer be concerned with looking inward. They must be concerned with what is taking place on neighboring lands. Nowdays, what occurs outside the parks' boundaries directly influences what happens to their internal resources.

Efforts have long been underway at Rocky to develop close ties with individual land owners, homeowner associations, developers, and businesses in both Estes Park and Grand Lake. This way the concerns of people both outside and inside the park can be known, understood and reflected in area planning. The park, utilizing a staff land-use specialist, seeks to influence development on private lands in such a way as to make it sensitive to the area's natural setting.

Cooperating with realtors in the Estes Valley, for instance, the park developed a brochure for new residents to heighten

...at Rocky Mountain National Park

awareness of concerns unique to living adjacent to a national park—such as maintaining seasonal migration corridors for wildlife, and using colors and housing materials that blend with the natural surroundings. In addition, the park works with neighboring landowners to produce practical guidelines for developing properties in such a way as to preserve the area's natural attributes. These efforts often equate to a longer and more complex process in achieving a consensus between the park and its neighbors. However, cooperation in the early stages of planning represents an efficient and economical approach toward achieving long-term regional and national resource goals.

The park's concerns over external impacts doesn't end with land development. Degradation of air quality resulting from urbanization, industry and mining from as far away as Southern California and Northern Mexico is of increasing concern. Water is affected as well because of the deposition of nitrates and other chemicals in the high country's winter snowpack. To meet its Congressional mandates to protect these resources, Rocky Mountain National Park, and other units of the National Park System, remain diligent in monitoring these impacts to natural resources-not only from the perspective of maintaining healthy park ecosystems, but to help neighboring jurisdictions maintain healthy, natural environments for their citizens.

In addition, the park is concerned with the impacts of increasing visitation on its natural,

archaeological and historical resources. Archaeological surveys and historical studies are underway as a precursor to developing strategies for protecting and preserving these remnants of past human activity. Since the early 1970s, a permit system to regulate overnight backcountry camping has been in place to mitigate human impact on vegetation and water resources. A shuttle bus system allows many more visitors to experience the breathtaking beauty of Bear Lake without having to pave natural resources near the lake for parking.

Continuing increases in the number of visitors to the park, and growing year-round use within the park (in part due to the mushrooming population in Colorado's Front Range communities), will challenge the park to devise effective, evenhanded systems for controlling public access. From its opening year (when 13,000 people entered its gates), to the 1990s (when over three million visitors had become the norm), the park's growing popularity has served as both a blessing and a bane to park administrators and employees. Balancing visitor use against resource protection continues as the park's highest priority into the 21st century.

New ways of funding research and park operations also will continue to receive high priority. By the summer of 1999, the park, in cooperation with private business, will have opened a much needed visitor center at the Fall River Entrance on U.S. Highway 34. The Rocky Mountain National Park Associates (a friends-of-the-park

group), and its cooperating association, the Rocky Mountain Nature Association, will continue to be relied upon to raise funds from the private sector. They will underwrite projects such as fully accessible trails, educational exhibits, and research and preservation projects. Congress, with its authorization of the Recreation Fee Demonstration Project, from 1997 through 1999, is working with the National Park Service to devise ways in which a larger percentage of entrance and camping fees may remain at the parks to reduce nagging maintenance backlogs. At Rocky Mountain National Park alone, this backlog is estimated at $54 million.

Most importantly, Rocky Mountain National Park and the National Park Service are committed to increasing public awareness of the national parks as part of the legacy belonging to all Americans. We who wear the "gray and green" are but the caretakers of some of our country's most spectacular natural areas and significant historical sites. These sites contribute to our uniquely "American Experience." Our goal is to increase society's understanding of the need for all Americans to enjoy our national parks but also to hand over, unimpaired, this irreplaceable legacy to our children and to our children's children.

Douglas L. Caldwell
Public Information Officer
Rocky Mountain National Park
January, 1998

Highlights of Nature

Alpine waterfall

E njoyment of nature is the primary reason to explore Rocky Mountain National Park. In a world that is becoming increasingly congested, it is a sanctuary for the soul, a delight for human senses. Here lie mountain peaks that glow pink with summer sunsets, whispering pines that skirt

gurgling brooks, soft grasses that wave beneath puffy-cloud skies and fragrant flowers that blossom by the meadow-full.

It is also home to an almost magical world of animals, birds and plants. Elk frequently make appearances, as do mule deer and bighorn sheep. Moose once again populate willowy valleys on the western side and black bear still roam the dark, subalpine forests. Songbirds and butterflies flutter above meadows and sage-dappled shrublands. Lazy summer days here are nothing short of sublime, as are the glistening vistas of winter, the colorful spectacle

of autumn and the budding promise of spring.

Occupying only a fraction of the 170-mile length of the Colorado's Front Range, the park displays the awesome effects of erosion and the classic features of glaciation. To see Rocky Mountain National Park is not only to gaze back into time, but to marvel at its incarnation as a wilderness monument for future generations.

Geology

Rocky Mountain National Park's geological history begins some two billion years ago. Thick accumulations of sand, mud, marine algae and

bacteria all fused under their own immense weight to form sedimentary rock—limestone, shale and sandstone. Around 1.7 billion years ago, metamorphic rocks such as gneiss, schist, marble and quartzites resulted from the motion of the earth's plates exerting intense pressure and heat on those long-buried sea sediments. Hot magma protrusions also periodically scorched the land and ocean floors and, as they cooled, created crystalline igneous rocks like granite and pegmatite.

Roughly 300 million years ago, the collision of the continental plates began an uplifting process, thrusting skyward a range of massifs now called the Ancestral Rocky Mountains. Millions of years of erosion reduced them to lowlands lapped by shallow seas and eventually, ancient oceans submerged them completely.

Eons passed as mud and sand again settled atop the once-grand mountains, forming more sedimentary rock. Then, approximately 70 million years ago, another era of uplifting began as the North American continent began to slide over the tectonic plate cradling the Pacific Ocean. Vast tracts of ancient rock were shoved and folded upward into north-south mountain ranges. Epochs of erosion gave way to volcanic eruptions, searing the terrain with molten lava, ash and pumice.

In more recent times, within the past two million years, a series of ice ages interspersed with warm, dry cycles have hewn Rocky Mountain National Park into the terrain we admire today. The most recent period of significant glaciation, starting about 28,000 years ago, nearly submerged the park with deep fingers of ice, 2,000 feet thick in some places. When the ice finally loosened its grasp, the "fingers" left in their wake moraines, hanging valleys, scooped-out cirques, jagged arêtes and towering, carved pinnacles.

Climate and Weather

Climate and weather refer to two different atmospheric conditions. Climate is the general meteorological nature of a region—its trends in temperature, precipitation and wind. Weather is the state of the atmosphere at specific times, taking into account variations in wind velocity, barometric pressure, moisture and temperature. In other words, climate is what to expect generally, while weather is what's happening today.

For the most part, the climate of Rocky Mountain National Park echoes that of Colorado: wet springs; hot, sunny summers with frequent afternoon thundershowers; warm, sunny and predominantly dry autumns; cold and snowy winters.

That said, the park experiences two distinct weather patterns, governed by the fact that high mountains divide the park from northwest to southeast. The ridges act as a barrier, so Western Slope weather is frequently much different from that of the Eastern Slope. During fall, winter and spring, Pacific air masses deliver rain and snow, along with occasional high winds, to the Western Slope. However, moist air masses from the Gulf of Mexico bring "upslope" conditions to the Eastern Slope, resulting in summer "monsoons," and during winter, occasional heavy snowstorms may occur. Sometimes an "Alberta Clipper" drifts down from Canada, bringing bitterly cold Arctic air.

Seasonal weather variations are also affected by the park's topography: its elevation, slope orientation and

Life-Giving Fire

Lightning-induced fires are natural forces in any ecosystem, and the forests of Rocky Mountain National Park depend on them. Surface fires consume dead wood, grasses and pine needles, removing thick layers of decaying vegetation. This enhances plant growth and replaces nutrients. In fact, lodgepole pine periodically require intense flame and heat. Their cones are sealed with dense pitch, and high temperatures are required to open them so their seeds can be released. Also, fresh ash invigorates the soil, producing an excellent seedbed. The result is a constantly regenerated habitat and an excellent food source for wildlife.

For the health of the forest, park officials maintain a Fire Management Plan. Its goal is to allow fire to play its natural role, while at the same time protecting life and property. Consequently, the forest service monitors and evaluates lightning-caused fires, permitting them to burn unhindered as long as they are within predetermined boundaries and meet specific criteria. Variables include projected fire behavior, current and forecasted weather patterns, fuel availability and smoke dispersal.

Occasionally, park personnel will also ignite fires to diminish ground fuels and restore forest conditions, but all unplanned human-initiated fires (and those that threaten people and property) are suppressed.

Natural fire, like rain, has its place in the environment, and can represent new beginnings rather than disaster.

Fall River Cirque near Alpine Visitor Center

exposure. As a general guideline, there is a three-degree-Fahrenheit drop in temperature for every 1,000 feet in elevation gain. Precipitation is more common in the higher altitudes and, because the air is thinner, ultraviolet radiation is far more intense. Sunburn can occur very rapidly here.

For planning purposes, it's always best to expect a wide fluctuation between day and night temperatures (up to 30° Fahrenheit), and to plan for sudden shifts during the day. The following guide summarizes the seasons:
- Spring (April and May): Rain is common in lower elevations, as is snow in the high country. Expect unpredictable changes from warm to cold and from wet to dry.
- Summer (June through August): Bright, warm mornings often give way to afternoon thunderstorms. Lightning is common, and it is essential to take adequate precautions against its dangers.
- Autumn (September through November): Clear, blue skies are the norm, with little overall precipitation and brisk temperatures. Toward late October and into November, snowshowers herald the beginning of winter.
- Winter (December through March): Crystalline, cold days prevail. However, sudden and intense snowstorms and blizzard conditions often exist. Deep snowpack covers the higher elevations.

Ecosystems

Only eight miles—as the eagle flies—separate the park's main entrances from the top of the Continental Divide. Nonetheless, the distance encompasses many worlds, ecosystems that range from dry montane forest to windswept alpine tundra.

While elevation is a crucial factor in determining what can and cannot survive in any ecosystem, several other influences also mark the habitats of Rocky Mountain National Park. Moisture accumulation and availability, slope orientation and soil composition also control the types of plants that will grow, and in turn, what animals will be supported by them. Rocky contains a diverse set of environments and supports hundreds of species of flora and fauna.

Rocky Mountain National Park contains four primary ecosystems:

Riparian

Situated along streams, rivers, lakes and ponds, riparian regions occur in both lower and higher elevations. Various shrubs—mountain and planeleaf willow, river and dwarf birch, and alder—thrive along well-watered shores. Beavers are the signature animal of these areas, although other mammals such as muskrats, river otters, raccoons, shrews and voles also call it home. Wildflowers abound, including chiming bells, mountain woodlilies and white bog

Missing Pieces of Mother Nature's Puzzle

Several animals that once roamed Rocky Mountain National Park no longer call its valleys, woodlands or alpine slopes home. The technical term for a species' absence is "extirpated," meaning that the animals were eliminated locally through hunting or trapping. These missing pieces of Mother Nature's puzzle include the grizzly bear and the gray wolf. In addition, the pronghorn and bison (buffalo) are known to have been pre-historical migrants, occasionally venturing into the park to feed. They no longer exist anywhere near the park. Further, animals such as the mink, wolverine and lynx have no recent confirmed sightings.

Ice Sculpture

The Rocky Mountain National Park of 20,000 years ago held a decidedly different terrain from the one we see today. This was the height of the last great Ice Age, often called the Pinedale Stage. More than three-quarters of the park's present acreage was submerged under immense glaciers. The Colorado River Glacier alone stretched for 20 miles down the Kawuneeche Valley.

Glaciers are referred to as "rivers of ice," for although they are frozen masses of water and incredibly heavy, they do actually flow. Over years of successive freezing and thawing, they travel forward and backward as snow accumulates and melts. With that motion, they sculpt the land, scouring out valleys, quarrying U-shaped troughs, bulldozing headlands and scraping flat, spacious pathways. Their distinctive touch is clearly seen throughout the park's clipped cliff faces, rounded basins and broad meadows. The following glossary identifies the major landforms that result from glaciers.

- Arête—Narrow, jagged spines, usually topping cirques.
- Cirque—Steep-walled, semi-circular basins appearing at the top of high valleys. This is where a glacier begins.
- Erratics—Huge boulders, once embedded in glaciers but left behind when glaciers recede.
- Hanging valley—These U-shaped troughs are smaller glaciers that flow into larger ones, forming a valley high on the wall of a bigger valley.
- Lateral moraine—Side ridges of debris and soil indicating the outer margins of an

Glaciers have shaped much of Rocky's dramatic landscape

advancing glacier.
- Terminal moraine—Headwalls of debris and soil marking the forward advance line of a glacier's snout.
- Roches moutonnées—Rocks too tough to be ground down by the glacier. These look like the rounded backs of sheep, hence their French translation, "sheep rocks."
- Tarn—Small, high mountain lakes formed in the bowls of cirques.
- Horn—A pyramidal peak formed by the intersection of several cirques.

The park's highest elevations, which remained glacier free, undergo their own cycles of freezing and thawing. When water freezes into ice, it expands. When present in the soil, water fractures stones and heaves rocks into piles of rubble. These "periglacier" areas bear the mark of frost action in several ways: Felsenmeer are fields of blocks scattered along ridges; "talus" are masses of rock debris scattered down a slope. "Patterned ground" appears as "rock polygons"—stones arranged in roughly geometric shapes surrounded by grassy areas—or "stone stripes," essentially rows of rock interspersed with lines of turf.

orchids. Birds nest and hunt here: American snipers, spotted sandpipers, Lincoln's sparrows and mallards.

Montane

Occurring between 6,000 and 9,500 feet in elevation, montane forests are relatively open terrain. Ponderosa pine prefer sunny, dry, south-facing slopes, whereas Douglas fir populate moister northern-aligned flanks. Lodgepole pine and aspen grow throughout the environment, often indicating areas of disturbance such as fire or avalanche, since both these tree species are quick to "pioneer" newly exposed terrain.

While many types of plants and animals range across the montane ecosystem, each tree type harbors communities that favor its company. Ponderosa parklands, for example, are the exclusive home of the Abert's squirrel, although mule deer, coyotes, striped skunks and porcupines also frequent the territory. Douglas fir are often interspersed with lodgepole pine, creating dense woodlands with thin understory environments. Shade-tolerant shrubs and flowers—common junipers, mountain maple, smooth asters, fairy slippers, dwarf mistletoe—shelter pine martens and red squirrels. Aspen glens form airier milieus, perfect for underbrush such as serviceberry, chokecherry and wild rose. Silvery lupines, yarrow and Colorado columbines dot the sunny areas where masked shrew hunt, and birds such as Cordilleran flycathers, violet-green swallows and downy woodpeckers dart from branch to branch.

Subalpine

Engelmann spruce and subalpine fir form dense forests from 9,500 to 11,500 feet. In disturbed areas, stands of aspen and lodgepole are common and on exposed rocky ridges, limber pine thrive. In the upper reaches, stunted, malformed trees called krummholz (German for "crooked wood") display the effects of strong winds studded with ice crystals. Heavy accumulations of snow and slow snowmelt keep the region moist. In the dark understory of the forest grow blueberries, huckleberries and elderberries interspersed with Jacob's ladder, red columbines and heart-leaved arnicas.

Least chipmunks and long-tailed weasels favor this cool environment, alive with the rustles, chirps and warbles of blue grouse, mountain chickadees, dark-eyed juncos and ruby-crowned kinglets.

High Altitude Pollution

Scientists have only recently started to study the effects of air pollution on Rocky Mountain National Park. For many years, toxic emissions from industry and automobiles were assumed to be problems confined to nearby urban areas, but now more than ever it seems that what goes up is coming down—into Rocky.

The park's pollution derives from several sources. First, there is automobile exhaust from cars along Colorado's rapidly developing Front Range which, if the wind direction is westerly, flows up into the park's valleys. In addition, thousands of vehicles ply the roads of the park itself, contributing to high emission levels.

Chemicals from car exhaust turn into ozone from a process involving sunlight. Over time, this could threaten animals and plants that are sensitive to higher levels of the gas. Sunlight also transforms emissions into haze, obscuring the views that are one of the hallmarks of the park.

Some specialists believe that Rocky is also adversely affected by the feedlots scattered amid the cattle-ranching centers along the northern Front Range. Cow manure emits high levels of ammonia gas and as this travels into the mountain air, it mixes with water from rain and snow, hitting the ground as ammonium nitrate. Nitrates then work their way into the soil, combining with other natural elements to increase the acidity of the water.

On a larger geographic scale, some researchers believe that wind-born pollutants from the Los Angeles Basin—1,000 miles to the southwest—also find their way to Rocky Mountain National Park. Chemicals, primarily nitrogen, are being deposited in the park, altering the composition of soil and water. Nitrogen is a key component of fertilizers, which can increase plant life along lakes and streams to create "eutrophic" water systems. Eutrophic waterways have nutrient mixtures that are too rich, spawning an over-abundance of algae and other plants, eventually altering the diverse natural habitat.

Elk and mule deer are common. Although this is their habitat, it is rare to come across black bears, lynx or wolverines in Rocky Mountain National Park.

Alpine Tundra

Above 11,500 feet trees disappear, giving way to an Arctic-like environment characterized by expanses of low-growing plants and fields of stone. This is the alpine tundra, where vegetation and animals must survive nearly 10 months of winter, often accompanied by hurricane-force winds.

It is far from a barren land, however. The short summer bursts into life with tufts of marsh marigolds, alpine phlox and fairy primrose, accented by grasses and lichens. Butterflies, such as high mountain blues and Magdelena alpines, seem too frail to occupy the windswept mountaintops, but they survive nicely. Horned larks and white-tailed ptarmigan also do well,

Golden eagle

staying clear of the hooves of elk and bighorn sheep or the busy antics of pikas and yellow-bellied marmots.

Wildlife Watching

Successful spotting of wildlife depends on many factors: the type of animal, understanding its habitat, the season, the time of day and most importantly, patience.

Wildlife watching also requires respect. With millions of people visiting the park annually, wildlife often come under severe stress from too many curious onlookers. Follow these simple guidelines to help preserve the park as a wild place.

- Never approach wildlife. Harassing animals is not only unlawful, but it causes them unnecessary anxiety.
- Admire wildlife from a distance. Sit down and keep a low profile. Use binoculars, spotting scopes or telephoto lenses to get close views. If

you're noticed and the animals seem nervous, you're too close. Move away slowly and quietly.

- Keep pets in the car. Dogs, in particular, will frighten animals. Also, pets can introduce diseases such as distemper.
- Drive slowly and watch for animals crossing the road. Deer, elk and bighorn sheep are seldom alone. If you see one, there are likely others close by. Stop your car to watch animals only if you can pull off the road safely. Do not block traffic.
- Talk quietly so you don't disturb wildlife or other people observing them. If you are in a car, turn off the engine.

Raptor Protection

Rocky Mountain National Park provides excellent habitat for birds of prey including Golden eagles, kestrels, turkey vultures, peregrine and prairie falcons, as well as red-tailed, Cooper's hawks and northern goshawks. Unfortunately, the rocky cliff faces where raptors prefer to nest and raise their young are also prime locations for adventurous rock climbers.

To ensure that raptors have safe—and undisturbed—nesting sites, wildlife managers have introduced protection programs, instituting closures of certain rock climbing areas at Lumpy Ridge and Sheep Mountain in March and April. Climbers should check with park personnel for details on dates and routes before heading to these areas.

Trees

Aspen

Banner trees

Ponderosa Pine

Aspen leaf

Ponderosa Pine
(Pinus ponderosa)
Ponderosa pines prefer sunny, dry, south-facing slopes in elevations up to 9,500 feet. Mature trees reach heights up to 100 feet with trunks three feet in diameter. Their shape is characterized by flat-topped crowns with long, swooping branches. Needles are three to seven inches long, grouped in bundles of two or three. Ponderosa pine bark is thick and reddish with a scent not unlike vanilla or butterscotch. Cones are woody with a short spine protruding from each scale.

Douglas Fir
(Pseudotsuga menziesii)
Found primarily in elevations up to 9,500 feet, Douglas fir prefer moist, north-facing slopes. Trunks are straight, with densely needled

upward-arching boughs—the perfect Christmas tree. Trunks have rough bark and can reach 30 inches in diameter, topping out at about 100 feet in height. Needles are one inch long, attaching singly to twigs. Cones are two to three inches long with distinctive three-pronged bracts projecting from between cone scales.

Quaking Aspen
(Populus tremuloides)
As "pioneering" trees, aspens are commonly found in areas that have undergone some disturbance such as a rock slide or fire. Aspen grow throughout the park but are usually found below elevations of 10,000 feet. They grow in groves and are exact clones of each other, as they propagate by sending out "suckers" or saplings from parents' root systems. Leaves are broad and paddle-shaped, and bark runs from light tan to green. It is often scarred with brown or black blemishes.

Lodgepole Pine
(Pinus contorta)
Lodgepole pine grows throughout the park, occurring in dense stands with tall, straight trunks reaching heights of 90 feet or more and diameters of approximately 18 inches. Needles are yellow-green in color, bundled

together in twos, and are one to two inches long. Cones stay attached to trees for years and are roughly two inches long. Native Americans harvested these trees for teepee construction, hence their name.

Engelmann Spruce
(Picea engelmannii)
Occupying elevations above 9,500 feet to treeline, Engelmann spruce have straight trunks and conical crowns. Trunks can be 30 inches in diameter and reach 100 feet with reddish- and gray-plated bark. One-inch-long needles are singularly attached to twig branches and one- to two-inch-long cones cluster in the top third of the tree.

Subalpine Fir
(Abies lasiocarpa)
Usually found in the same range as Engelmann spruce, the Subalpine fir is narrower in shape with denser foliage. They grow to 80 feet in height, have trunks with diameters of 28 inches or more, and bark that appears smooth and silvery. Needles are flat, slightly curved with rounded tips and are singly attached to branches. Cones grow upright on the uppermost branches and are somewhat purplish in color. They are rarely found on the ground.

Red and White Flowers

Fireweed

Indian Paintbrush

Calypso Orchid

RED FLOWERS

Fairy Slipper or Calypso Orchid
(Calypso bulbosa)
Named "Calypso" for the nymph of Homer's *Odyssey*, this delicate flower favors decaying wood for its germination and flowering, and it is often seen sprouting in lodgepole pine forests. Late spring and summer is its blooming period, when single, pink-petaled blossoms with large, scoop-like lips rise from a single glossy leaf.

Fireweed
(Epilobium angustifolium)
This pioneering flower is often the first plant to come up in sites disturbed by fire. Tall stems have narrow leaves, and the flowers themselves spike out from the top in showy bursts of multiple petals. More than 25 species of fireweed exist in the Rockies, and sometimes the common variant is also called "Blooming Sally."

Scarlet Indian Paintbrush
(Castilleja miniata)
Paintbrush hybridize easily and there are more than 200 species ranging in color from red to purple to white. They are members of the figwort family, and their petals are essentially bracts encompassed by tubular flowers. Although common in natural areas, they are difficult to nurture in landscaped gardens.

Elephantella
(Pedicularis groenlandica)
Also called "Little Red Elephants," the name stems from their shape, which resembles a pachyderm head and snout. Their comical construction aids in pollination as the "trunk" gently buffets bees' abdomens while the insects drink nectar. Look for herds of elephantella along wet stream beds and lake shores.

Shooting Star
(Dodecatheon radicatum)
With distinctive reverse-pointed petals and yellow nose cones, shooting stars bud upward, then plunge groundward while in bloom. They thrive in wet areas from montane to tundra, blasting

Red and White Flowers

Mariposa Lily

Wild Tiger Lilies

Alpine Phlox

off from narrow stems attached to rosette bases.

WHITE FLOWERS

Alpine Phlox
(Phlox condensata)
A deep taproot allows the alpine phlox to hug the windswept reaches of the alpine highlands. Mature specimens explode with dainty flowers during the brief summer. Native Americans once used these to cure digestive ailments.

Bedstraw
(Galium boreale)
Used as a mattress filler in the olden days, its hooked leaf and stem corners helped prevent bunching. It has a sweet scent, and the seeds were sometimes

ground and served as a substitute for coffee. The montane zone is its habitat, where it tolerates sunny, dry areas. It thrives best, however, in moister zones.

Cow Parsnip
(Heracleum sphondylium ssp. montanum)
Related to the carrot, this giant flower can reach seven feet and its spectacular umbrella-like flower heads stretch more than a foot across. Cows do eat it, as do other wildlife, but humans find the taste bitter. Another pitfall: it closely resembles water hemlock –deadly if consumed.

Mariposa Lily
(Calochortus gunnisonii)
Mormon pioneers were saved

from starvation by eating this plant; all its parts are edible, especially the bulb. A look-alike, the sego lily, is now the Utah state flower. The word *mariposa* means butterfly in Spanish, and indeed, the flighty creatures are one of the flower's primary pollinators.

Pearly Everlasting
(Anaphalis margaritacea)
Like fireweed, pearly everlasting is quick to propagate in recently burned areas. Their bead-like blossoms do appear like bunches of pearls and stay this way even after they are plucked and dried. Remember, though, picking wildflowers on park grounds is not only illegal, it also destroys the habitat.

Bluebell

Colorado Blue Columbine

Forget-Me-Not

BLUE FLOWERS

Alpine Forget-Me-Not
(Eritrichum aretioides)
Hugging rugged scree slopes in the tundra, forget-me-nots are among the first flowers to bloom in short high-country summers. Their intense blue coloring holds anthocyanin, a chemical pigment that helps convert light to heat, thus enabling them to withstand freezing temperatures.

Colorado Blue Columbine
(Aquilegia caerulea)
Although nine species of columbine are found within Colorado, the blue variety is the official state flower. Related to buttercups, its fancy "spurs" are reservoirs for sweet nectar, a favorite of hummingbirds. In the late 1800s, wildflower gathering was popular among tourists and nearly decimated the flower. The Colorado Mountain Club worked to protect it and in 1925, a law was passed enforcing the Columbine's conservation.

Mountain Harebell
(Campanula rotundifolia)
This may be one of the most common wildflowers in the Rockies, flourishing in both low altitudes and at treeline. Their pretty drooping flowers are fashioned like little bells, hence the Latin name *campanula*. Actually, their sleepy-looking shape helps protect their pollen from the elements.

Tall One-sided Penstemon
(Penstemon virgatus)
There are more than 250 species of penstemon in North America and several varieties are common in the Rocky Mountains. This one-sided variety gets its name from the arrangement of its flowers, which tend to hug one side. They can grow to more than a foot high and are frequently seen along roadsides or in meadows where animals often graze.

Silvery Lupine
(Lupinus argenteus)
A member of the pea family, lupines look like bluebonnets and have many hybrids. They range throughout the park, but are most common in subalpine

Blue and Yellow Flowers

Yellow Pondlily

Yellow Lady's Slipper

Black-eyed Susan

areas amidst lodgepole pine and sagebrush highlands. Upon maturity, seeds become widely scattered by the wind as their pods burst open with forceful pops.

YELLOW FLOWERS

Black-eyed Susan
(Rudbeckia hirta)
Commonly seen along trails and roadsides, the black-eyed Susan's dark center is slightly cone-shaped and becomes more so as the seeds mature. The Swedish botanist and originator of modern plant taxonomic classification, Carolus Linnaeus (Carl von Linné), named this far-ranging flower in honor of two botanists, a father and son who shared the name Claus Rudbeck.

Heartleaf Arnica
(Arnica cordifolia)
An old name for heartleaf arnica was "leopard's bane" and indeed, no one has seen this feline in Rocky Mountain National Park—ever. The flower itself resembles a daisy, and is common to moist subalpine forest. Stem leaves are paired and heart-shaped, a feature that differentiates this species from the 14 other types of arnica found in the Rockies.

Western Wallflower
(Erysimum asperum)
Wallflowers are members of the mustard family and during wet springs, they carpet montane meadows with showy bouquets. Some species of wallflowers

actually grow well near walls, and their name was thus applied to shy young girls who also preferred the shelter of walls at social events. Wallflowers are sometimes referred to as "blister cress," for their pungent juice has been used to heal skin burns.

Yellow Pondlily
(Nuphar luteum)
Floating atop shallow lakes, the yellow pondlily's large roundish leaves help keep ponds cool and habitable for fish and other aquatic species. Ducks eat their seeds and muskrats, their long rootstalks. Native Americans also ate their seeds, which taste similar to popcorn.

Birds

Red-tailed hawk

Golden eagle

Bluebird

American Kestrel
(Falco Sparverius)
Formerly referred to as the sparrow hawk, these are the smallest members of the falcon family. They are present throughout the year, often hovering in mid-air in search of small rodents and insects. Males have bluish wings, females are more russet. Both display rust-toned tails and two stripes on their heads.

Clark's Nutcracker
(Nicifraga Columbiana)
These bluish-gray birds are gregarious, and are often seen at pullouts and other observation points looking for scraps of food.

When left to their natural feeding patterns, they favor limber pine nuts, which they pry out and store for the long winter. The birds don't recover all their horde, and many seeds germinate to foster the regeneration of limber pines.

Golden Eagle
(Aquila chrysaetos)
Dark brown in color, these large birds display golden-hued feathers on the napes of their necks. From high altitudes they scan for rodents and other small mammals, swooping down to clutch prey in their powerful talons. Pairs mate for life, and use the

same nesting site year after year.

Mountain Bluebird
(Sialia Currucoides)
Male mountain bluebirds are brilliant blue with pale blue underbellies. Females are less colorful, grayish with blue tails. They nest in tree cavities, and both parents look after four to six hatchlings. They prefer higher altitudes and are often mistaken for western bluebirds, which dwell at lower elevations.

Mountain Chickadee
(Parus Gambeli)
These commonly seen birds stay year-round in conifer forests, nesting in old tree stumps.

Birds

Owl

Ptarmigan in summer

Raven

Predominantly gray and white, they are identified by their white eyebrows and black bibs. During the chill of winter, they fluff out their feathers to create air pockets for insulation.

Red-tailed Hawk
(Buteo Jamaicensis Calurus)
This is by far the most common hawk in North America, and is usually spotted soaring over open fields and meadows, where it hunts small rodents. As its name implies, a distinctive red tail is the way to quickly identify it, but its long piercing whistle is also a clue to its presence.

Raven
(Corvus corax)
The raven is considered a songbird, but its cry is more like a throaty croak. Heavy and all black, ravens are successful scavengers and therefore help keep forests clear of carrion. They are frequently confused with crows, which look similar but don't display the wedge-shaped tail that distinguishes ravens.

Red-naped Sapsucker
(Sphyrapicus Nuchalis)
Red-naped sapsuckers are woodpeckers with bright red patches on their throats and heads, and white stripes above and below their

eyes. Perching on vertical tree trunks, they drill holes and return later to collect the sap and insects which accumulate.

Steller's Jay
(Cyanocitta Stelleri)
Seen throughout the year, these distinctively cobalt-blue birds with showy head crests frequent picnic areas; they love to panhandle for castoff food bits with noisy cries. They don't need to beg, however, for they are consummate food gatherers, thriving on forest seeds, berries and insects. During the month of May, look for them high in treetops where they nest, hatching clutches of chicks by June.

Large Mammals

Mule deer

Moose

Bull elk

Bighorn Sheep
(Ovis canadensis)
Both males (rams) and females (ewes) have horns. Rams sport the heavy, curlicue variety while the ewes grow short, slightly curved ones. Sometimes females are mistaken for mountain goats. However, bighorn sheep have tan or dark brown coats, and goats are white. Bighorn sheep prefer rocky slopes, although they frequent lake areas where there are nourishing mineral deposits.

Black Bear
(Ursus americanus)
Black bears can be black, but they are just as likely to be cinnamon brown. Weighing between 200 and 600 pounds, they are smaller and less aggressive than their cousin, the grizzly bear. Although they are carnivores, black bears feed primarily on nuts, roots and berries.

Coyote
(Canis latrans)
Known for their eerie howling at sunset, coyotes are generally shy, highly adaptable animals. They range throughout the park, opportunistically feeding on small mammals, birds, plants and even the occasional amphibian. Only rarely will coyotes team up to bring down larger mammals such as deer or elk.

American Elk
(Cervus elaphus)
Also called *wapiti*,—a Native American word meaning "white rump"—these majestic animals are mostly brown, with a darker head and shoulders. Autumn heralds the beginning of the mating season, when bulls (some weighing 1,000 pounds with five-foot-long antlers) gather harems of cows. "Bugling"—a plaintive sort of whine—is used by males during the rut to announce their presence.

Large Mammals

Coyote

Mountain lion

Red fox

Mountain Lion
(Felis concolor)
These tawny brown cats can weigh as much as 200 pounds and have the strength to bring down much larger deer and sometimes elk. After killing their prey, they eat heartily and then hide the remains under leaves, returning several times over the course of many days to feed again. Largely nocturnal and sparsely distributed, they are seldom seen.

Moose
(Alces alces)
Standing seven feet tall at the shoulder and weighing over 1,200 pounds, moose are the largest members of the deer family. Their favorite environment is the marshy area along streams and lakes, where they utilize their long legs to wade in the shallows for willows and other aquatic vegetation.

Mule Deer
(Odocoileus hemionus)
Large mule-like ears give the mule deer its name. Weighing approximately 200 pounds, they are heavier than their relatives, the white-tailed deer. November is their mating season, and it's not uncommon to see males challenging each other by locking antlers in twisting and shoving matches. After rut, males shed their antlers, which sprout again in the spring.

Red Fox
(Vulpes vulpes)
Strikingly beautiful with rich orangey-red coats and fluffy white-tipped tails, red foxes are small, timid animals. They usually weigh less than 15 pounds. Small mammals such as mice, rabbits and squirrels are their favorite, though it's possible to see them pouncing through meadows chasing large insects.

Small Mammals

Least chipmunk

Yellow-bellied marmot

Raccoon

Abert's Squirrel
(Sciurus aberti)
Easily spotted due to their signature tufted ears, Abert's squirrels don't hibernate; they remain active during the winter. Ponderosa pine forests are their habitat. They nest in treetops and feed on the cones and the inner bark of young twigs.

Beaver
(Castor canadensis)
Perhaps no other animal profoundly alters the landscape like beavers do. Their dam construction ability can change a free-flowing stream into a pond within a matter of days. Here, they erect lodges using aspen, willow and alder as building material.

Golden-mantled Ground Squirrel *(Spermophilus lateralis)*
Named for their gold-colored heads and necks, they also sport light-colored stripes running up their dark-toned backsides. Consummate beggars, golden-mantled ground squirrels are quite habituated to human presence. They find plenty of food in the wild, however, storing nuts, seeds and berries in underground burrows.

Least Chipmunk
(Tamias minimus)
Frenetically active, least chipmunks can be identified by white stripes, which run along their cheeks on either side of their dark eyes and down their backs. They fatten on seeds and berries during the summer, then hibernate in the winter in underground burrows.

Northern Pocket Gophers
(Thomomys talpoides)
Although they are rarely spotted, the presence of northern pocket gophers is easily detected. Look for low mounds of freshly dug earth in meadows and fields. Pocket gophers are relentless burrowers. Their name comes from the cheek pouches in which they stuff food while foraging.

Small Mammals

Pika

Golden-mantled ground squirrel

Red squirrel

Pika
(Ochotona princeps)
Pikas are small members of the rabbit family and live in the rocky slopes of subalpine and alpine ecosystems. Since they don't hibernate, they spend their summer days foraging in meadows for greens, storing hordes of food amidst the crevices of their stony sanctuaries.

Porcupine
(Erethizon dorastrum)
Noted for its clever protection system—some 30,000 or more five-inch-long quills—porcupines never seem to be in a rush. Few predators take them on. Porcupines feed on sprouting plants in the spring and summer and in the winter, they eat the inner bark of trees.

Red Squirrel / Chickaree
(Tamiasciurus hudsonicus)
Bushy-tailed and boisterous red squirrels seem to chatter constantly as they busy themselves with finding sufficient cones to devour during the winter. Discarded husks and cone fragments become their "midden"; large piles of refuse form a natural blanket over their winter nests.

Snowshoe Hare
(Lepus americanus)
The way to tell a snowshoe hare from a cottontail is to look at the hind legs. Snowshoe hares have rather large feet. During the summer, snowshoe hares are brown in color, but in the winter they molt, growing pure white coats that easily camouflage them in snowfields.

Yellow-bellied Marmot
(Marmot flaviventris)
Called "whistling pigs" for their distinctive high-pitched squeak, yellow-bellied marmots claim the alpine talus slopes for their home. They spend summers feasting on sprouting plants, adding nearly 60 percent to their total body weight to survive long winters of hibernation.

following pages: left: Bighorn sheep; right, bull elk

Rocky Mountain Recreation

Trail ride at Moraine Park

For Rocky Mountain National Park, the words "wilderness preservation" and "recreation" are two sides of the same coin. The park presents countless opportunities for fishing, hiking, snowmobiling, horseback riding, camping, climbing and snowshoeing. Yet the park's rangers are often in a conundrum: As well as maintaining the park as an out-of-doors playground, they bear the responsibility to protect the natural and cultural resources of this wilderness jewel. This balancing act requires the participation and foresight of both park officials and park visitors.

Over the years, park managers have had to face numerous challenges to preserve the integrity of ecosystems while welcoming millions of annual visitors. At times, this has meant strict regulations, and occasionally, the complete removal of popular attractions in order to restore threatened habitats; Moraine Park once held a nine-hole golf course, and until 1992, Hidden Valley sported a ski resort.

Decisions to restrict public access and certain activities are never taken lightly. Park management relies on the counsel of numerous experts and concerned citizens to ensure that this wondrous region continues to be loved—but not loved to death. It is, after all, a place that represents freedom and space, where one can indulge in nature's pleasures, whether that be hiking up a magnificent "14er" or lazing away an afternoon near a babbling brook.

Ultimately, it's up to the users of the park to tread lightly upon it: to stay on trails, to carry out trash, to avoid the temptation to feed begging critters, to leave wildflowers in their place, to go gently so others may follow.

Hiking

More than 350 miles of trails traverse through Rocky Mountain National Park, making hiking the most popular activity of the area. Detailed trail maps, available at the park visitor centers, outline options ranging from easy nature trails with little vertical elevation gain to strenuous ascents of the park's alpine peaks. In addition, the Larimer County Parks Department, the U.S. Forest Service, the National Park Service, the Town of Estes Park and the Estes Valley Recreation and Park District have developed a 170-mile system of interconnecting trails that provide access to Rocky Mountain National Park and the Roosevelt National Forest; contact the Larimer Country Parks Department at 970-679-4570.

Rocky has many trailheads, each offering walks and hikes of varying lengths and difficulties. Visitors looking for an "easy" hike or a walk might think of hopping on the shuttle for Bear Lake. Several short, easy yet spectacular hikes originate from this activity center. Sprague Lake offers a wonderful, light-on-the-legs walk around the lake. The nature trail at the Moraine Park Museum is simple, and simply loaded with views. Adams Falls, east of Grand Lake, is a deep forest walk that rewards hikers with a view of a splendid waterfall and a lovely meadow.

Winter snows restrict hiking in the park during the chilly season; particularly west of the Continental Divide, which receives heavier amounts of precipitation. On the eastern side of the park, snowfall is usually lighter, leaving several lower elevation trailheads open: The Pool, Cub Lake, Chasm Falls, Gem Lake, Deer Mountain and Upper Beaver Meadows. While skis or snowshoes aren't

Camping in the wilderness

A Hiker's Checklist

Hiking safely means being prepared. Rapidly changing weather, injuries or unfortunate encounters with wildlife can quickly turn a pleasant outing into a nightmare. Use the following checklist as a things-to-bring starter kit that will help in unforeseen circumstances.

- Extra clothing; layering is always the best strategy for fickle weather. Don't forget raingear.
- Plenty of food and water. Also, consider water-purification tablets in the event that potable water is not available.
- All-purpose knife, with scissor and tweezer functions
- Sun protection, including a hat or visor, sunglasses and sunscreen lotion
- Insect repellent
- First-aid kit
- Matches in a waterproof container, plus a firestarter candle and/or chemical fuel
- Compass and map of the area
- Flashlight with fresh batteries
- Whistle for signaling if lost
- Space blanket

Hiking Rocky Mountain National Park

Trailhead/ beginning elevation (feet)	Hike name	Difficulty	Distance (miles, one way)	Elevation gain (feet)
Bear Lake (9,475)	Nymph Lake	Easy	0.5	225
	Dream Lake	Moderate	1.1	425
	Emerald Lake	Moderate	1.8	605
	Lake Haiyaha	Moderate	2.1	745
	Bierstadt Lake	Moderate	1.6	255
	Lake Helene	Moderate	2.9	1,215
	Odessa Lake	Moderate	4.1	1,205
	Sprague Lake Five Senses	Easy; specifically designed for disabled visitors	0.5	Level
Bierstadt Lake (8,500)	Bierstadt Lake	Moderate	1.4	566
Colorado River (9,010)	Lulu City	Moderate	3.1	350
Coyote Valley (8,846)	North Valley View	Easy, wheelchair accessible	0.5	0
Cub Lake (8,080)	Cub Lake	Moderate	2.3	540
Deer Ridge Junction (8,930)	Deer Mountain	Moderate	3.0	1,083
East Inlet (8,391)	Adams Falls	Easy	0.3	79
Fern Lake (8,155)	The Pool	Easy	1.7	245
	Fern Falls	Moderate	2.7	645
	Fern Lake	Moderate	3.8	1,375
Finch Lake (8,470)	Finch Lake	Moderate	4.5	1,442
Gem Lake (7,740)	Gem Lake	Moderate	2.0	1,090
Glacier Gorge Junction (9,240)	Alberta Falls	Easy	0.6	160
	Mills Lake	Moderate	2.5	700
	The Loch	Moderate	2.7	940
Green Mountain (8,800)	Big Meadows	Moderate	1.8	606
Lily Mountain (8,780)	Lily Mountain	Moderate	1.5	1,006
Longs Peak Ranger Station (9,300)	Eugenia Mine	Moderate	1.4	508
North Inlet (8,540)	Cascade Falls	Moderate	3.5	300
Rock Cut (12,110)	Toll Memorial	Moderate	0.5	200
Sprague Lake (8,710)	Around Lake	Easy, wheelchair accessible	0.5	20
Twin Owls (7,920)	Gem Lake	Moderate	1.8	910
Wild Basin Ranger Station (8,500)	Copeland Falls	Easy	0.3	15
	Calypso Cascades	Moderate	1.8	700
	Ouzel Falls	Moderate	2.7	950

Difficulty levels are based on trail distances, elevation gain, beginning elevations, hiker reactions, ranger recommendations and the origin of visitors.

In addition to the easy and moderate hikes listed, Rocky has many hikes that are considered strenuous. Confer with a park ranger for more information.

necessarily required, extra precautions should be taken as winter weather conditions can change rapidly. Always check with park personnel for current trail conditions and avalanche warnings before heading out.

Camping

Rocky Mountain National Park has five drive-in campgrounds: Aspenglen, Glacier Basin, Longs Peak, Moraine Park and Timber Creek. In addition, Sprague Lake Handicamp offers camping opportunities for physically challenged nature lovers.

All campgrounds are equipped with piped cold water and toilets, but there are no shower facilities. Only ice and firewood are available for sale; there are no provisions of any kind. With the exception of Longs Peak, recreational vehicles are accepted, though none have hook-up facilities for water, electricity or sewer. Pets are allowed in the camps, but they must be leashed at all times. While the park can accommodate nearly 600 campers, many additional tent and RV sites are also located in Estes Park and Grand Lake. See chapters five and eight for private camping facilities at Estes Park and Grand Lake, respectively.

Camping in Rocky is quite popular during the summer months and reservations are encouraged. Bookings are taken for Moraine Park and Glacier Basin Campgrounds— the park's largest—through DESTINET, P.O.Box 85705, San Diego, California, 92186-5705; 800-365-2267. The other campgrounds are available on a first-come-first-served basis.

Winter camping is available at Moraine Park, Timber Creek and Longs Peak.

Backcountry Backpacking

Reservations are required to spend the night in any backcountry areas in the park. Permits can be obtained at the park headquarters, Kawuneeche Visitor Center and, during the summer months, at the Longs Peak and Wild Basin ranger stations. Maximum night restrictions apply and reservations are required from May to mid-August. They cost $10. Call 970-586-1242 for more information.

Camping Within Rocky Mountain National Park

Campground RV Sites	Tent/	Cost	Open / Day Limitation	Reservations
Aspenglen	54	$12/night	Open year-round; 7 day max. stay*	First come, first served
Glacier Basin	150	$14/night	Open June to September	Reservation required June to September; 800-365-2267
Longs Peak	26 tent sites; no RVs	$12/night	Open year-round; 3 day max. stay*	First come, first served
Moraine Park	247	$12 non-reserved; $14 reserved; $10 during winter	Open year-round; 7 day max. stay*	Reservation required Memorial Day to September; 800-365-2267
Sprague Lake Handicamp	Backcountry tent camping for 12 people	$15 permit fee	Open Summer and Fall; 3 day max stay	Reservation required; 970-586-1242
Timber Creek	100	$12/night	Open year-round; 7 day max. stay*	First come; first served

* Parkwide camping is limited to seven nights from May 22 to September 30. An additional 14 nights are permitted from October 1 to May 21. At Longs Peak Campground, a three-day limit applies between May 22 to September 30.

Fishing

A Colorado State Fishing License is required to fish the streams and lakes within the park. Children under the age of 12 may use bait in waters that are not catch-and-release designated; all others must only fish with flies and artificial lures. Only common shanked (barbless) hooks are permitted and the fishing season is year-round, 24 hours a day, except in certain areas such as Hidden Valley Beaver Ponds. Eight is the possession limit, and of that total, six must be brook trout. The others may be rainbow or brown trout at least 10 inches in length. In addition, a bonus of 10 brook trout is allowed, provided they are less than eight inches in length.

For the protection of native greenback cutthroat and Colorado River cutthroat trout, some waters within the park are closed to fishing, while others are catch-and-release with barbless hooks only. In particular, Bear Lake is closed to all fishing and Lily Lake is catch-and-release only. For locations of open lakes, streams and other closed waters, consult park personnel before fishing. Brochures are available at visitor facilities.

Outside Rocky Mountain National Park, different rules apply. A fishing license is still required, and only one rod may be used unless a second rod stamp is purchased. Except for live minnows, bait may be used in most waters. Up to three common shanked hooks may be employed. Fishing season is year-round, 24 hours a day. Adults may take eight fish, and children under the age of 14 may keep four;

Responsible Recreation

"Take only pictures, leave only footprints" may sound like a cliché, yet the phrase captures the spirit of what responsible recreation entails. Each of us shares an obligation to leave the beauty of Rocky Mountain National Park unblemished by our presence, and if possible, to improve its current condition. Here are easy ways to help achieve that goal.

Follow the Rules

Each year, park officials print thousands of leaflets to inform visitors of how they can help preserve the pristine wilderness. These regulations are designed to maintain ecosystems and, in many cases, to protect humans from danger.

Do Not Feed the Animals

Feeding animals discourages their natural foraging habits. Whether they are cute chipmunks or curious birds, they have been fending for themselves for generations without the intervention of humans. True, all animals face lean times now and again. That's nature's way. Moreover, animals bite and can easily mistake a fingertip for a tidbit, transmitting diseases in the process.

Don't Pick the Flowers

Tempting as it may be to pluck just one beautiful bloom as a remembrance of a beautiful day spent in the park, wildflowers need to be left to grow and seed. They won't be back next year, or for future generations, if they're harvested for temporary bouquets.

Stay on the Trails

For the most part, hiking trails have been established within the park to accommodate the vast numbers of people who come here to enjoy its scenic splendor. They have been carefully planned and arranged to make areas accessible and at the same time, to lessen the impact of humans' venturing into wild habitats. Occasionally, a quicker route presents itself. However, "shortcuts" not only jeopardize the integrity of the landscape by needlessly damaging vegetation, they also place hikers crossing unstable terrain at risk.

Pick Up and Pack Out

Even after decades of hearing "Don't be a litter bug," it's amazing to see that people still think nothing of tossing away gum wrappers, cigarette butts and other scraps. Take the ethical high ground by carrying along a litter bag for your own trash, but also as a way to collect those cast-offs you find along the way. The park will be a much cleaner, prettier place if we all pitch in.

Respect the Nature Experience of Others

Excessive shouting and garrulous laughing have their place, but not while a group of people are absorbing the magic of watching a timid group of bighorn sheep or strutting elk. Also, hiking paths are everyone's nature highway, places for both slow pokes and power walkers. Be considerate of your fellow hikers' paces, move aside graciously, and never set up picnics in the middle of the trail.

Wrangler at Glacier Creek Stables

no size limitations are imposed except in posted areas.

Several waters carry special regulations, including the Big Thompson River (from Waltonia Bridge to Noels Draw), North St. Vrain River, Lake Granby, Grand Lake, Shadow Mountain Reservoir and Button Rock Reservoir. Current rules are available from the Colorado Division of Wildlife (303-297-1192). General fishing information is available at 303-291-7533, and the stocking report at 303-291-7531.

Finally, for fishers who want to try waters with a better-than-average chance of a catch, private fishing operations exist in Estes Park. No license is required, all gear is supplied, catches are frozen and stored or, if you prefer, grilled on site. See chapter five for specific operators.

Horseback Riding and Pack Animals

Approximately 260 miles of the park's trail system are open to equestrians and pack animals including mules, burros and llamas. Deer Mountain, Horseshoe Park, Moraine Park, Glacier Basin and Emerald Mountain are the primary zones open to horses and pack

animals, and in these areas, nearly 80 percent of the trails are equipped with hitchracks. In addition, park concessionaires offer several scenic half-day and day-long saddle trips, guiding visitors to Beaver Meadows, Mill Creek, or along the old Ute Trail. Call Glacier Creek Stables at 970-586-3244 in the Sprague Lake area, and Moraine Park Stables at 970-

First Aid

No matter how short the outing, a well-stocked first aid kit is an essential companion. Stores in both Estes Park and Grand Lake stock a variety of commercially packaged kits, or you may wish to construct your own. Here's a checklist of items to include:
- First-aid instruction book
- Adhesive bandages in a variety of sizes
- Large-sized (4x4 inches) sterile gauze pads
- Sterile adhesive tape
- Antibiotic ointment
- All-purpose pain reliever (such as aspirin)
- Antiseptic swabs and alcohol pads for cleaning wounds
- Elastic bandages for sprains
- Moleskin for blisters
- Tweezers or scissors, or a Swiss Army knife with these tools
- Space blanket

586-2327 for the Moraine Park area. Also, there are several livery operations in the Estes Park area, as well as at Grand Lake; see chapters five and eight.

For people who plan to bring their own stock into the park for recreational use, several regulations apply, including but not limited to the following:

- Overnight camping requires a permit, which is obtained in advance. Stock camps have designated areas and reservations are highly recommended.
- All stock must use existing trails; no cross-country or off-trail travel is permitted. Horses and other stock are not permitted on park roads, with the exception of certain sections necessary to reach trailheads. Llama users must yield the trail to horses and other stock animals when passing.
- Horses and other stock are not allowed in campgrounds or picnic areas. Galloping of horses and other stock animals is not permitted within park boundaries. Use of stock-drawn equipment is not allowed.
- Loose herding is not permitted and all stock must be under physical control at all times. Grazing is not permitted; feed must be packed in.

Climbing

Rock climbing is a treat in Rocky Mountain National Park, as it offers great bouldering and challenging technical ascents. No permit is required unless you stay overnight. The best place to see climbers practicing belays is on the south face of Lumpy Ridge in the MacGregor Park area north of Estes Park. For climbing information and lessons, contact the Colorado Mountain School (CMS) in Estes Park at 970-586-5758, a private enterprise specializing in climbing.

Choosing a Hike

With more than 50 designated hiking trails within Rocky Mountain National Park, choosing which hike to take can be as challenging as the hike itself. Here are a few tips to consider before you lace up your hiking boots.

Looking for Serenity? If you're after peace and quiet, you will want to get an early start. Many trails become crowded rather early. Late afternoon treks can also offer serenity.

Looking for Wildlife? If wildlife viewing is your goal, early morning or late evening hikes hold the best chance of spotting creatures both large and small.

Want to Go Alone? Hiking alone is never recommended; if you find yourself in a jam, there is no one to help you.

Want to Hike with Others? While you may want to conquer a five-mile strenuous route, it's certainly not wise to push children or those with physical limitations to match the pace. Avoid frustration by discussing the options before you head out.

Know Your Physical Limitations. Hikes in the park range from easy-going strolls with little elevation gain to strenuous routes that will test the mettle of experienced mountaineers. Plus, the altitude of many trails can take their toll. Take it easy for the first few days.

Choose Your Views—Rocky offers many ecosystems and visual splendors to see. Here are some easy hikes—walks, really—with specific goals in mind.

The View You're After:	The Place to Go:
Craggy peaks and lakes	Bear Lake
Riparian habitat	Fern Lake, Cub Lake
Easy hikes	Sprague Lake, Bear Lake, Beaver Ponds Boardwalk
Subalpine ecosystem	Bear Lake
Ponderosa parklands/Montane ecosystem	Moraine Park, Horseshoe Park
Alpine tundra	Tundra World Nature Trail
History	Never Summer Ranch, Lulu City
Riparian habitat	Fern Lake, Cub Lake
Fish and beaver	Beaver Ponds Boardwalk
Waterfalls	Alberta Falls, Copeland Falls, Calypso Cascades, Adams Falls

Cycling

All hiking trails are off limits to bicycles. Therefore, the only cycling routes follow the principal roads in the park: Bear Lake Road, Trail Ridge Road and a loop in Horseshoe Park. No fee is required other than the standard park entrance charge for cyclists. Heavy vehicle traffic is common, and bikers should prepare for unpredictable weather and high altitude.

Bear Lake Road climbs 1,500 feet from U.S. Highway 36, ending at Bear Lake at an elevation of 9,475 feet above sea level. The road is narrow, with nearly continuous traffic during the peak hours of the day. Trail Ridge Road is a grueling climb, rising nearly 4,000 feet to the Alpine Visitors Center at 11,796 feet. Significant vehicle traffic, cool temperatures and gusty winds accompany riders. The Horseshoe Park/Estes Park Loop is best tackled by heading west on the U.S. Highway 34 Bypass via the Fall River entrance. At Deer Ridge Junction, proceed east on U.S. Highway 36 through the Beaver Meadows entrance, terminating at Estes Park.

Both Estes Park and Grand Lake have bicycle rental providers. In Estes Park, contact Colorado Wilderness Sports at 970-586-6548 or Colorado Bicycle Adventures at 970-586-4241. In Grand Lake, call Rocky Mountain Sports at 970-627-8124.

Rafting and Kayaking

Rafting and kayaking are not permitted within Rocky Mountain National Park.

However, several rafting outfits operate out of Grand Lake, taking participants on whitewater excursions of the nearby Colorado River. Estes Park also has rafting companies, offering float trips of the Cache la Poudre River. See chapters five and eight for details.

Swimming

In a word: don't. Mountain water is exceedingly cold, quickly inducing hypothermia—the condition that results when the body is too chilled to warm itself adequately. Further, *giardia lamblia*, a tiny protozoan, thrives in the streams and lakes. Diarrhea, cramps and bloating are the nasty effects that accompany giardiasis. Don't drink the water.

Cross-country Skiing / Snowshoeing

From December to May, moderate to deep snow blankets the valleys and ridges of Rocky Mountain National Park, creating perfect terrain for cross-country skiing and snowshoeing. Park ranger-led cross-country ski tours depart on Saturdays at the Kawuneeche Visitor Center. Ranger-led snowshoe hikes leave from Bear Lake on Saturdays and Sundays.

Numerous self-guided trails, from beginner- to advanced-level, originate at Bear Lake, Glacier Gorge, Glacier Basin and Wild Basin on the park's east side, and on the west side of the Continental Divide at East Inlet, North Inlet, Tonahutu Creek, Green Mountain, Onahu Creek and along the Colorado River.

Several trails are marked with fluorescent orange markers, but on longer routes, navigation will require the use of a compass and topographic maps. Further, many ski touring trails originate in the areas surrounding both Estes Park and Grand Lake.

Remember, outdoor winter recreation requires planning and adequate precaution to avoid the dangers of severe weather and avalanches.

Snowmobiling

Trail Ridge Road from the Kawuneeche Visitor Center north to Poudre Lake is a designated snowmobile route. Snowmobilers are required to register at the visitor center before entering the park. The route is shared with vehicle traffic and is kept plowed as far as the Colorado River Trailhead. While in the park, all Colorado snowmobile and use regulations apply. Traffic and regulatory laws are enforced by park officials. All routes are clearly marked, and travel up snow banks and through meadows or outside established routes is prohibited. The turn-around area at Milner Pass is posted, and no snowmobile traffic beyond this point is allowed. Snowmobiling is prohibited on the east side of the park.

Grand Lake has several snowmobile rental shops, as well as many routes within the area. See chapter eight for specific snowmobile information. Call 970-586-1333 for park road and weather information and 970-586-9561 for additional weather information.

Estes Park

Longs Peak with Estes Park in the foreground

W hen Joel Estes and his party emerged from the confining walls of the Big Thompson River Canyon in 1859, the breadth and beauty of this large, level meadow—or "park," as these areas are called— took his breath away. "We were monarchs of all we surveyed," he is

recorded to have said. "We had the world to ourselves."

Many of today's travelers have a similar reaction, for the setting—despite considerable development—still drops jaws. On the south rises Prospect Mountain. To the west, the silvery-with-snow, ragged-topped pinnacles of Colorado's Front Range aim skyward. A glimpse to the north reveals the unusual and appropriately named formations of Lumpy Ridge.

History

Estes wasn't the first to admire the area. Ute and other native peoples had been hunting mountain bison (now extinct) in these environs for centuries. Evidence suggests that Oldman Mountain west of town was once used as a site for spiritual quests. And while the Arapaho nation claimed the land as their own, it was the Ute who were occupying it when the first settlers arrived.

In addition to his name, Estes left behind quite a legacy. While he, his wife and their 13 children came to ranch, they found it hard going at 7,500 feet above sea level. Estes

moved to richer land in New Mexico, but not before he and other struggling ranchers discovered the region's true calling as a haven for hunters and travelers.

In fact, *Rocky Mountain News* publisher William Byers rented rooms from Estes himself on his first exploration to the area in 1864 to climb Longs Peak. Though Byers failed to reach the summit, his story about the adventure honored his host by referring to the region as Estes Park.

The mountain climbing bug bit Byers hard and he

left: Wild rose bushes in the town of Estes Park

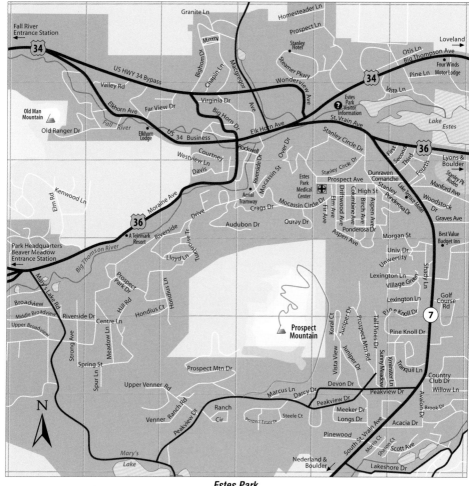

Estes Park

convinced Major John Wesley Powell, the famous Colorado River explorer, to climb Longs Peak with him. This time, they made it to the top and the article Byers published began to draw visitors to Estes Park from around the world.

One Irish nobleman and hunter—Windham Thomas Wyndham-Quin, Fourth Earl of Dunraven, Viscount of Mount Earl and Adare—was so taken with the area that he conspired to buy up every homestead. His idea was to keep his illegally acquired 15,000 acres for himself and his favored associates as a hunting and fishing paradise. Luckily, honest homesteaders got the better of him.

But the region's destiny had been set in stone. Many ranchers found themselves renting out rooms and gradually adding lodges and building restaurants. F.O. Stanley, co-inventor of the Stanley Steamer, came for the benefit of his health and ended up spending the next 37 summers. In 1909, he built the inn that bears his name; The Stanley Hotel is the famous setting of the book, movie and TV mini-series, *The Shining.* More importantly, Enos Mills—cowboy, miner, hotelier and self-taught naturalist—arrived, settled in and before long was lobbying to set aside expansive tracts of land for a national park. Beginning in 1909, Mills traveled the country, lecturing and writing about the Rockies. In 1915, his efforts were rewarded with the establishment of Rocky Mountain National Park.

Layout

Each of the three roads leading into Estes Park offers drop-dead gorgeous views on the way into the valley. Colorado Highway 7 comes in high from the south with views of Marys Lake and Prospect Mountain. U.S. Highway 36 ribbons in from the east, capturing overlooks of Lake Estes itself. Finally, U.S. Highway 34 climbs through the same sheer-walled canyon that Estes struggled out of in 1859.

These roads all converge on Estes Park, squeezing hundreds of cars into the five-block length of Elkhorn Avenue before diverging again on the west side of town. During late July and August, Elkhorn and the roads leading in and out of town often clog with many of the park's three million annual visitors.

There are ways of finding relief. The U.S. Highway 34 Bypass (Wonderview Avenue) provides an outlet for folks heading west out of town toward the park's Fall River Entrance Station. Visitors aiming for the Beaver Meadows Entrance Station or Park Headquarters (with its visitor center)

Annual Estes Park Festivals and Events

November to April
Sunday afternoon Concerts at the Historic Stanley Hotel; presented by the Estes Park Music Festival; 2 p.m.; free; 970-586-3371.

February
Valentine's Day Weekend/Romance in the Rockies; renewal of vows, sweetheart dance and romantic activities; 800-443-7837.
International Dog Pull; competition on snow and bare ground; 800-443-7837.

March
Women's History Month; art and museum exhibits; 970-586-9203.

May
Jazz Fest & Art Walk; self-guided tours and non-stop free jazz; 970-586-6140 or 970-586-9203.
Duck Fest; thousands of plastic duckies racing down Fall River for charity, prizes and music; 970-443-7837.
Parade of Years Old Time Car Rally; from Loveland to Estes Park; 970-586-6256.
Big Horn Challenge; run for charity; 970-443-7837.

June, July
Nightly Cowboy Sing-alongs; around the campfire in Bond Park; downtown; 970-443-7837.
Lazy B Wranglers; stage show

and chuckwagon supper; 970-586-5371.
Music in the Mountains; chamber music at Rocky Ridge Music Center; 970-586-4031.

June
Annual Wool Market; largest animal fiber show in the country; 970-586-6104.
Scandinavian Midsummer Festival; celebrates summer solstice; 970-586-9203.

July
July Fourth Fireworks over Lake Estes; fireworks; 970-443-7837.
Estes Park Music Festival; Colorado Music Festival Orchestra; 970-586-9203.
Rooftop Rodeo and Parade; downtown and Stanley Park Fairgrounds; 970-586-6104.
Hunter Jumper Horse Shows; Stanley Park Fairgrounds; 970-586-6104

August
SummerFest; free concerts at YMCA of the Rockies; 970-586-3341.
Christian Artists Music Seminar; 800-755-7464.
Lake Front Arts Fest; visual work; music, dance, theatre; 970-586-9203.
Best of West Estes Brewfest; 970-586-5421
Westernaires in Performance;

horse-riding displays; 970-586-6104.

September
Labor Day Crafts Show; Bond Park downtown; 800-443-7837.
Longs Peak Scottish Highland Festival; four-day-long celebration of all things Celtic, pipe bands, dance competition, food, crafts, folk music; 800-443-7837.
Fine Arts and Crafts Show; juried fine arts show; 970-586-9203.
Autumn Gold; Octoberfest-style celebration; 800-443-7837.
Merchant's Surprise Sale; 800-443-7837.

November
Catch the Glow Christmas Parade and Celebration; 800-443-7837.
Annual Holiday House; Christmas bazaar; 800-443-7837.

December
Annual Holiday Home Tour; 800-443-7837.
'Round the Table Sing; chorale concert; 970-586-9203.
Celebrate the Season; fireworks, carolers, hayrides; 800-443-7837.
Holiday Open House; Estes Park Area Historical Museum; 970-586-6256.
Estes Park Oratorio Society; Messiah sing-along; 970-586-9203.

may turn south onto Riverside Drive, which skirts much of downtown and follows the Big Thompson River along its less-settled south bank. Then, turn north one block on Marys Lake Road and back onto U.S. Highway 36, also called Moraine Avenue.

Elkhorn Avenue is not simply crowded because it's the only street that runs through town, it is also the heart of the shopping and restaurant neighborhood. Dozens of retail stores run along both sides of Elkhorn, offering everything from books and postcards to pizza and beer. Benches, old fashioned lightposts and plantings help screen shoppers from the traffic. Large lots provide plenty of parking at each end of downtown, so visitors may park and walk to enjoy the downtown's five-block length.

Most of the hotels, condominiums, cabins, lodges and motels in Estes Park string along the roads that lead into and out of town.

Visitors Center

The Estes Park Visitor Information Center (970-586-4431 or 800-443-7837) anchors the intersection of U.S. Highways 36 and 34. Open during the summer, Monday to Saturday from 8 a.m. to 8 p.m. and Sunday 9 a.m. to 6 p.m., the center offers a variety of services. Volunteers are on hand to answer questions and make hotel and excursion reservations. In addition, a wall of brochures provides handouts on everything from campgrounds to fly-fishing clinics.

Contemporary Aspects

Estes Park is a village caught

Children's Activities in Estes Park

- An easily accessible playground is located on the river's edge where East Riverside Drive crosses the Big Thompson River. Plenty of parking is available, as are restrooms.
- The Estes Park Public Library (970-586-8116), located at 335 East Elkhorn Avenue (at MacGregor Avenue) has an excellent children's area. Children may sit here to read, or visitors may borrow books after receiving a temporary library card. Check out the group storytelling times.
- There are two movie theaters in Estes Park: The Stanley Village Cinemas (970-586-4227) and the historic Park Theater (970-586-8904).
- Fun City (970-586-2070) has putt-putt golf, video games, go-carts, a water slide and bumper cars.
- Trout Haven (970-586-5525) offers fishing in a well-stocked pond.
- Pony rides are available at the Elkhorn Lodge (970-586-4416), at Cowpoke Corner Corral (970-586-5890) and at National Park Village Stables (970-586-5269).
- Several stores cater to children: Geppettos (970-586-5709) and Mountain Zoo (970-586-2160) are both located in the heart of Elkhorn Avenue shopping area.
- Rocky Mountain National Park has an almost unlimited number of educational programs for kids. For a listing, consult the *High Country Headlines*, available at visitor centers and ranger stations in the park.

between nurturing one of the nation's most superb natural wonders and meeting the demands of its guests. It has been

Facts on Floods

Recently, Estes Park has suffered two devastating floods.

On July 31, 1976 after several days of intermittent rain, 12 inches of water poured onto Estes Park in a four-hour period. The ensuing flood raged down the Big Thompson River Canyon, sweeping 145 people to their deaths.

Some folks, racing down the canyon in their cars at breakneck speeds, were overtaken by the water and drowned. This explains the signs in Big Thompson Canyon to climb to safety in case of flooding.

The Lawn Lake flood of 1982 resulted from the failing of the Lawn Lake earth dam in the mountains of Rocky Mountain National Park. On the morning of July 15, thousands of gallons of water escaped the dam, wreaking havoc as it tore through the Aspenglen Campground killing three people and causing millions of dollars of damage to downtown Estes Park. Much of Elkhorn Avenue, which shoppers enjoy so much today, was buried in water and mud.

Aerial Tram at Estes Park

criticized in the media and by environmentalists as being over-developed and "touristy."

In truth, the vast majority of the three million annual visitors to Rocky Mountain National Park pass through Estes Park in the 90–95 days between Memorial and Labor days. That adds up to several thousand new visitors arriving every day, each with individual needs. Satisfying them is a daunting task that this city of 8,000 accomplishes with friendly efficiency.

While Estes has its detractors, the fact is that since the Lawn Lake flood of 1982, which ravaged Elkhorn Avenue, the city has come a long way toward making the visitor's experience more pleasant. Trees, benches and plantings line the avenue now, and along the river stretches a

delightful park with flagstone walks, bronze sculptures, shaded benches and playgrounds for children. A recreational pathway connects the heart of downtown to the visitor center and continues on to a lakeside hiking and biking trail.

Accommodations

The quintessential Estes Park accommodation is a quaint and cozy log cabin with a tiny kitchen and a porch trimmed out with log handrails. Interiors tend to feature knotty pine with furniture running the gamut from cast-offs to fine oak. Log-rail porches sport rockers. These cabins always seem to be scattered among similar cabins, usually under a gnarled Ponderosa pine or two. Often, a creek or river flows past them. Indeed, the closer the cabin is to water, the higher the room rate. These bungalows give a wonderfully rustic feel to a western vacation.

More recently, many motels and condominiums-for-rent have sprung up along the roads heading into Rocky Mountain National Park. These, too, tend to log-cabin styling, but with more updated interiors and amenities. Many have kitchens.

The primary four-month visitor season makes running a hotel in Estes Park a financial challenge. Holiday Inn, Best Western and Comfort Inn operate the only chain properties in town. Perhaps the best-known hotel is the Stanley, with its Georgian-style architecture and stunning views.

Camping in Estes Park

Campground	Tent/RV Sites	Season
Estes Park Campground 970-586-4188	68	May 22 to mid-September
KOA 970-586-2888 or 800-562-1887	100	April 25 to mid-October
Marys Lake Campground 970-586-4411 or 800-445-MARY	150	May 1 to September 30
Manor Trailer Park 970-586-3251	98	May 15 to September 30
National Park Resort 970-586-4563	150	May 1 to September 30
Paradise Travel Park 970-586-5513	30	May 1 to October 1
Yogi Bear's Jellystone Park 970-586-4230 or 800-722-2928	105	Mid-March to September 30
Spruce Lake RV Park 970-586-2889	110	April 1 to mid-October
Blue Arrow Campground 970-586-5342 or 800-582-5342	157	April 1 to October 1

Stanley Hotel

When Freelan Oscar Stanley was constructing the hotel that bears his name in 1907, he discovered that he alone would be responsible for bringing in the utilities and services—the local power company wasn't up to the task. Luckily, Stanley was. He had, after all, co-invented a dry-plate printing process that brought him $1,000,000 a year until he sold it to George Eastman of Kodak. And he had co-invented a steam-driven automobile— the Stanley Steamer—that was making him another fortune. So designing and building the first electric kitchen in the country, and a hydroelectric plant to run it, didn't present much of a challenge.

Stanley was determined to build in Estes Park. He had come from Massachusetts to take the cure for tuberculosis: the bone-dry, high-altitude air. The remedy seemed to be a success. Stanley arrived in Denver in March, 1903, visited Estes Park three months later and kept coming back for 37 years.

One of the first things Stanley noticed was that there were plenty of rustic ranches to stay in, but nothing luxurious. Consequently, Stanley and his partner, B. D. Sanborn, bought 6,400 acres from the Earl of Dunraven in 1905 and started construction on the hotel. Much of the lumber used was felled and sized in nearby Hidden Valley but more exotic woods and supplies were brought overland more than 20 miles by horse teams.

The Stanley Hotel

The guests were conveyed from Lyons as well, but not by pack animal. Paying customers found themselves enthroned in specially designed, steam-driven "mountain wagons" and driven up to the front door in style. An introductory tour included the MacGregor Dining Room (serving continental cuisine and spectacular views), the Music Room (where the ladies might enjoy the hand-carved Steinway concert grand), the Piñon Room (cigars and liquor for the men) and one of Stanley's favorites, the Billiard Room (where he is said to have once insisted that a guest leave the hotel because the visitor had found fault with Stanley's bank shot).

Before long, the well-to-do of the time were arriving to savor the Wild West in high style.

Personalities such as "Molly" Brown, John Philip Sousa and Theodore Roosevelt took part in the recreation offered: bowling, billiards, horseback riding and sightseeing drives up Old Fall River Road.

But none of this explains why the Stanley is so well known today. The hotel's fame nowadays stems from a visit many years ago by author Stephen King. Indeed, King got the idea for the eerie happenings of his novel *The Shining* during a stay in the Stanley in the 1970s. It must have been quite a visit.

Despite rumors, film director Stanley Kubrick's movie version was not shot here but on sets in England. However, when King himself decided to remake the piece in 1996, he returned to the original rooms that had haunted him so. And no, the hotel does not close during the winter.

The Shining isn't the Stanley's only claim to fame. It showed up as an Aspen, Colorado, property in the Jim Carrey movie *Dumb and Dumber*, and has welcomed guests such as singer Peter Gabriel, astronaut Scott Carpenter and M*A*S*H's Radar, Gary Burghoff. The Emperor and Empress of Japan dropped in for lunch in 1994.

Today, the Stanley Hotel (970-586-3371 or 800-976-1377) serves northern Colorado as a hotel and conference center with 133 rooms and more than 15,000 square feet of meeting space.

Restaurants

As you might expect in a region that hosts millions of guests each year, the restaurant scene serves up everything from cotton candy to gourmet specialties. Restaurants have learned the lesson of diversity: offer a wide selection. It's not unusual to see Italian, Mexican, American and German items all on the same menu. Several restaurants offer dishes such as elk, trout and bison.

Shopping

Though barely a half-mile long, downtown Estes Park has dozens and dozens of stores housed behind a diverse group of facades. But what a range of products are offered: kites, clothing, maps, magnets, cameras, old-time photographs, T-shirts, candy apples, rocks, fossils, plaster dinosaur castings, candles, stamps, perfume, jewelry, fine art, Native American art and leather goods. One of the oldest stores, the Taffy Shop, has been dispensing salt-water taffy to generations of Estes Park visitors since 1935.

Attractions

Beyond the shadow of a doubt, the prime attraction in Estes Park is the neighboring Rocky Mountain National Park. Virtually thousands of visitors spend every day in Rocky, coming into Estes Park only for meals and a room. Most, however, take a day or two away from the wilderness and wildlife to explore the attractions around town.

Many begin at the Aerial Tram (970-586-3675). Completed in 1955, the tram whisks passengers from a base elevation just above the Big Thompson River (at 7,800 feet above sea level) nearly to the top of Prospect Mountain—a gain in elevation of 1,100 feet. The ride takes a mere 3.5 minutes. The cheery and cherry-red cars, which run every five minutes, are suspended from more than 2,600 lineal feet of cable pulled along at 1,200 feet per minute by a 75-horse-power motor.

All this makes for a smooth-as-silk ascent, accompanied by views of nearly all of Estes Park. At the top, riders disembark for a hike to the peak of Prospect Mountain—a moderately steep, one-mile walk on gravel road. Others take the half-mile scenic stroll through forest and rocks to a western overlook. Many buy a bag of peanuts at the gift shop—which has a clean-as-a-whistle cafe, too—to feed the insistent squirrels.

Across Riverside Drive from the tram rises the multi-colored water slide of Fun City (970-586-2070). This amusement park features a group of activities that are perfect for children and tends to be busiest in the evening. They have a bumper car track, a putt-putt golf course, a water

A Day or So in the Park

It's possible to get a good feel for Rocky in only a day—but it will be a busy one.

First, stop in at Park Headquarters to study the scale model of the park and guage the lay of the land. Next, pay a visit to the Moraine Park Museum for an hour to study the exhibits on glacial effects and flora and fauna that the park contains in such abundance. Then, head for the Glacier Basin parking lot to catch the shuttle to Bear Lake. Take a leisurely stroll around the lake and enjoy the scenery. Next, head north to Horseshoe Park and drive up Old Fall River Road (no trailers or vehicles longer than 25 feet are allowed). Enjoy this tightly wound road with its interesting stops, and in all likelihood, a wildlife spotting or two. After a rest at the Alpine Visitor Center, head back to Estes Park via Trail Ridge Road, pausing at the various overlooks.

With another couple of days in the park, be sure to add a walk and a picnic at Sprague Lake or take the short climb up to Alberta Falls, and spend some time in Grand Lake. Head down the Kawuneeche Valley, stop at the pulloffs to learn about Grand Ditch, the Continental Divide and the Never Summer Ranch. Spend a night in Grand Lake, paddle a boat around the lake itself, savor lunch at the Grand Lake Lodge and stretch your legs on the easy hike to Adams Falls or the meadow above the falls.

With several days to enjoy the area, be sure to spend a day strolling around Estes Park. Elkhorn Avenue is a fun place for shopping; fishing the Gold Medal waters of the Big Thompson River is a treat for serious fishers. A stop at Sheep Lakes might yield a bighorn sheep sighting, and longer hikes such as the easy (but long) walks into the Eugenia Mine or Lulu City reward with terrific scenery.

slide and video games. Across a small bridge runs a go-kart track.

The Estes Park Area Historical Museum (970-586-6256) honors turn-of-the-century speed demons with its display of Stanley Steamers. Other exhibits explain the lifestyles of a previous century: those of beaver trappers and Native Americans. A general store presentation explains shopping way-back-when and in the back yard, cabins and wagons give a sense of what life must have been like for the ranchers and farmers who settled this area. The original Rocky Mountain National Park headquarters building—a white clapboard structure—acts as a gallery for changing exhibits. A book shop sells a variety of history-related materials and a five-minute video provides an overview of the region.

One of the most historic homes in the area is the Mac-Gregor Ranch. In the shadow of Lumpy Ridge, this house-museum displays the down-home lifestyle of a well-to-do ranch family. It's so authentic, you expect to see dirty dishes in the sink.

Put the Baldpate Inn (970-586-6151) in the authentic category, too. Their lunch and dinner buffets are renowned in the area. So is their key collection; they display nearly 20,000 keys in a log-lined room near the dining room.

Two other private businesses in Estes Park are so distinctive and so popular that they deserve mention as attractions. The first is Dick's Rock Museum (970-586-4180). The owners of this shop on

U.S. Highway 36, about four miles east of Park Headquarters, have been polishing, cutting and selling every kind of rock and stone imaginable for years. This is the splendid, dusty kind of shop that rock hounds love. The other is primarily for kids, but parents love to watch their kids love it. At Trout Haven (970-586-5525), hundreds of fish fill a pool nestled near the Big Thompson River. The Haven provides rod, reel and bait, which participants use to reel their dinner out of the pond. They'll clean and ice the catch, charging by the inch or, for an additional few dollars, they'll fry it up and provide all the fixings.

Recreation

In addition to the many recreational temptations of Rocky Mountain National Park, Estes Park has a few outdoor prizes of its own.

Golfers seem to like the fact that balls travel up to 15 percent farther in this high altitude. Invariably, elk join golfers in the autumn at the two courses in town: Estes Park Golf Club (970-586-8146) is a public, 18-hole, par 71 course located two miles south of downtown on Colorado Highway 7 ; the Lake Estes Executive Course (970-586-8176) lies along the lake near the Big Thompson River and all that water makes even this flat course a bit tricky.

Maybe it's better to aim for the water with a fishing lure. Lake Estes is stocked with rainbow trout. The Lake Estes Marina (970-586-2011) rents boats and sells tackle. The Big Thompson River east of Estes Park, right along U.S. Highway 34, is one of Colorado's hottest fishing spots; stocked

Why So Many Parks?

Colorado is full of parks: Estes Park, North Park, Middle Park, South Park, Moraine Park, Hollowell Park. None of these refer to shady, lawn-carpeted acreage, however, but to geological features found in the mountains. Generally, the term "park" describes any broad, grassy, flat area surrounded by mountains or hills. The word is derived from the French word, *parque,* meaning "enclosure."

There are three types: North, South and Middle Parks are immense bowl-shaped basins formed over millions of years. Here, areas of the earth's crust that were dozens of miles in diameter dropped as the surrounding mountains rose.

Moraine Park and Hollowell

Park were actually formed by glaciers. As 2,000-foot-deep ice rivers headed downstream, they transformed the valleys from V-shaped gouges into gentle U-shaped valleys. Gravel pulled up by the ice churned to the sides, forming high ridges called moraines. This resembles the way the dirt is moved aside while plowing. These ridges, and the valley itself, can be clearly seen from the Moraine Park Museum.

Estes Park resides in a different kind of park altogether. This area is essentially a valley that gradually filled up with sediment that was washed out of the mountains over thousands of years.

Bighorn sheep sculpture

rainbow and brown trout put up a good fight from May to September.

The Colorado Mountain School (970-586-5758) offers classes covering nearly every kind of climbing: crack, face and anchor. They offer one- to seven-day climbing camps that teach beginners how to conquer the hills. After winter storms, they get out their crampons and axes and dig into ice climbing.

Since Rocky Mountain National Park doesn't allow off-road bicycling, cyclists often leave town a touch frustrated. Not to worry, the Roosevelt National Forest offers plenty of fun, particularly on four-wheel-drive roads. For rentals, try Colorado Bicycling Adventures (970-586-4241) or Colorado Wilderness Sports (970-586-6548).

American Wilderness Tours (AWT) (970-586-4237) uses some of these same roads on their day-long or sunset four-wheel-drive adventures. Guests pile into their vehicles, go for the ride of their lives on steep terrain, and have a meal in a forest overlook that AWT maintains in the nearby Roosevelt National Forest.

Swimmers are welcome during open swimming at the Estes Park Aquatic Center (970-586-2340). A small fee is charged.

The Elkhorn Lodge (970-586-4416) bills itself as Colorado's oldest continuously operated hotel. While they offer guest-ranch-style extended stays, they also provide dudes or dude-wannabes the opportunity to sling a leg over a horse and go for a ride amid the splendors of the Colorado wilderness. Aspen Lodge (970-586-8133), a comfortable conference center with views of Longs Peak, will saddle up folks for a ride as well.

Nightlife

Most folks are plain tuckered out by the end of the day, so the nightlife in Estes is somewhat limited. Low-stakes gambling is allowed in Central City, a 55-mile drive south on Colorado Highway 7, the Peak to Peak Scenic and Historic Byway. The Lazy B (970-586-5371 or 800-228-2116) rustles up chuckwagon suppers with western-style entertainment every night. The Stanley Hotel (970-586-3371) offers classical concerts many weeknights and weekends. Summer moviegoers get a kick out of the fun but decidedly funky Park Theater (970-586-8904), one of the oldest movie theaters in the state.

MacGregor Ranch

When Alexander MacGregor visited these parts in 1872, he fell in love with both the land and another visitor, Maria Clara Heeney. Two years later, MacGregor homesteaded acreage and married Maria. Their children left Estes Park, but a granddaughter, Muriel MacGregor, grew up on the ranch and ran it until she died in 1970.

No spot in Colorado better illustrates the life of reasonably well-to-do-ranchers than the MacGregor Ranch Museum (970-586-3749). The stone and log house is packed to the roof with furniture, dishes, art, sports equipment, riding gear and all the other items a family collects over a hundred years. The museum is open from 10 a.m. to 4 p.m., Tuesday through Friday during July and August.

following pages: Sprague Lake

Vistas and Vales

Mt. Ypsilon

Not all of Rocky Mountain National Park is gnarled peaks and rugged tundra; most of it is quiet valleys astir with elk and deer, gurgling streams roiling with fish and ridge upon ancient ridge bristling with forest and atwitter with birds. It is in these vales that we stand to admire those vistas. On these ridges, we sense the grandeur of those peaks.

Rocky seems to present two halves: the alpine wonder on high and the playground down below. While the high country may be the reason to come and gaze, the lower elevations are the reason to come and play. Rocky's lower elevations accommodate lakeside strolls, gentle hikes to watery flumes, horseback rides, Gold Medal fishing, historic homes and museums and a rare feeling of wilderness and connectedness to nature.

Sculpted by millions of tons of frozen water thousands of years ago, the sheer-sided valleys here were ground into the flat-floored parkland meadows we see today.

Glaciers acted like plows furrowing fields into enormous rows. Like a plow, those glaciers left earth pitched up on either side. These ridges—called lateral moraines—divided the land vale from vale. Several such valley parklands grace the lower elevations: Horseshoe Park, Upper Beaver Meadows, Moraine Park and Hollowell Park. But not every glacier carved a park; some dipped only a little way down their mountain's side, forming basins such as Glacier Basin and Wild Basin.

Horseshoe Park/Deer Ridge

Two roads splay out of Estes Park, heading into Rocky Mountain National Park. The U.S. Highway 34 Bypass heads north around Oldman Mountain, paralleling Fall River and entering the park at the Fall River Entrance.

U.S. Highway 36 loops past Oldman on its south, rises in elevation to achieve a breathtaking vista of Longs Peak and

left: Hallett Peak

enters the park, after passing the Park Headquarters, at the Beaver Meadows Entrance. This pair of two-lanes comes together after looping through Horseshoe Park and riding the shoulder of Deer Ridge.

Park Headquarters Visitors Center

Rocky Mountain National Park's stunning headquarters building, which serves also as a visitor center, occupies an inviting, low-slung, concrete-and-steel structure designed by Taliesin Associates, the heirs to Frank Lloyd Wright's architectural heritage. Very much in Wright's style, the center hugs the ground, local stone forms rampart-like walls and a triangular, earth-red steel structure echoes the massive summits beyond.

Inside, a variety of services helps acquaint visitors with the park. A plaster model explains the park's shape and terrain; lights twinkle on and off, illustrating the locales of the park's highlights. Park rangers answer questions from behind a counter strewn with maps. The answers to many inquiries are contained in the *High Country Headlines*, the park's free newspaper. An excellent book store sells books, postcards and calendars. Nearby is a rack of brochures that the park itself distributes containing detailed information on such topics as wildlife, hiking, forest fires and the alpine tundra. Downstairs in the auditorium, a 20-minute film orients viewers to Rocky's many delights.

Beaver Meadows Entrance Station

In the summer months, the large meadows before and after this entrance station fill the air with the earthy fragrance of wildflowers. Coyotes are often seen in these open areas.

The high ground to the north after the park entrance is the lateral moraine of debris left by the Bull Lake glaciation thousands of years ago.

Upper Beaver Meadows Trailhead

A gravel road heading west leads to the Upper Beaver Meadows trailhead. This area offers access to Ute Trail,

Enos Mills Cabin

"I'm Enda Mills Kiley," says the woman sitting in the corner of the log cabin, "I'm Enos Mills' daughter."

It is rarely as simple to get to the source of history as it is at the Enos Mills Cabin. Still owned and opened to the public by Mills' family, the Enos A. Mills Cabin Museum and Gallery (970-586-4706) takes visitors on a fascinating trip back to the beginnings of Rocky Mountain National Park.

Mrs. Kiley or her daughter frequently staff the 10x10 foot cabin with its stunning view of Longs Peak. They happily recount the story of Mills, the man who homesteaded here in 1885 and wrote, lectured and lobbied so strongly for the formation of Rocky Mountain National Park that he is considered the father of the park.

which winds its way up-valley and eventually onto the tundra itself. Upper Beaver Meadows provides superb views of the Front Range, along with excellent wildlife viewing in the morning and evening.

Beaver Meadows Overlook

From the overlook here, the strand of peaks that forms the

southern quarter of the Front Range is simply incredible. From Mount Meeker, the skyline spikes up and down all the way to Stones Peak. In the foreground, the cadence of sequential valleys and ridges, typical of Rocky's glacier-carved eastern side, advances southward.

Deer Ridge Junction

This intersection of U.S. Highway 34 and U.S. Highway 36, which was once a developed area of hotels, is now the decision point between heading west across Trail Ridge Road or turning north into Horseshoe Park.

Deer Mountain Overlook

A small turnout on the east overlooks Deer Mountain. Below, in Little Horseshoe Park, the first Civilian Conservation Corps compound west of the Mississippi River set up camp. Known as the "Woodpecker Army" because they were hauled to work in bright red tour buses, the 200 men stationed here did landscaping, pulled out dead trees and built trails.

Horseshoe Park Overlook

From this single spot, much of Horseshoe Park's story may be told. To the left burrows the Fall River Valley from which flowed the river of ice that leveled Horseshoe's floor. Above Fall River climbs the Mummy Range: Mounts Chapin, Chiquita and Ypsilon are visible. The massive mound dead ahead is Bighorn Mountain, which is aptly named given that its rocky escarpments frequently host bighorn sheep. The eastern horizon is spiked with the slender stone piles of the Lumpy Range, home to falcons and eagles.

Sheep Lakes Overlook

The cluster of silver lakes glittering in the green of this healthy riparian ecosystem is Sheep Lakes. Such ponds formed when glacial ice actually dug holes in the ground

Montane Ecosystem

Elevation: 7,500 to 9,500
Description: Because of variations in flora and fauna, this ecosystem is broken into two bands. Lower Montane systems typically have widely spaced Ponderosa pine trees on sunny, grassy, south-facing slopes and Douglas fir on cooler, wetter faces. Upper Montane areas grow aspen and lodgepole pine.
Microclimate: Temperatures vary from well below 0° to 90° Fahrenheit; plant types are very sensitive to variations in available sunlight and water.
Tree types: Aspen, lodgepole pine, Ponderosa pine, Douglas fir.
Where to go: Moraine Park is a classic Lower Montane ecosystem. Trail Ridge Road from Deer Ridge Junction west to Many Parks Curve passes through an Upper Montane ecosystem.
Undergrowth types: Juniper, sagebrush, kinnikinnik, berry bushes
Animal types: Coyote, chipmunk, mountain chickadee, Stellar's jay, porcupine, red squirrel, bobcat, deer, elk.
Wildflowers: Fescue, paintbrush, many grasses, heart-leaved arnica, clematis.

Riparian Ecosystem

Elevation: These habitats occur at a variety of elevations; plants and animals differ, depending on elevation.
Description: Riparian areas form a separate ecosystem within the Upper and Lower Montane ecosystems. They are quite common in Rocky; look for moist, overgrown areas alongside rivers and lakes. The lush water-dependent habitat attracts many animals.
Microclimate: Depends on location.
Tree types: Aspen are common, as are blue spruce, narrow-leaved cottonwood and balsam poplar, depending on elevation.
Where to go: Big Thompson River in Moraine Park, Upper Horseshoe picnic area, Kawuneeche Valley.
Undergrowth types: Willow, alder and birch bushes; chokecherry, shrubby cinquefoil.
Animal types: Moose, trout of many varieties, American dippers, garter snake, beaver.
Wildflowers: Cow parsnip, bittercress, chiming bells, sedge grasses.

that fill with water yearly.

Soils around these lakes brim with salts that the bighorn crave. After their limited diet in the winter, sheep come here almost daily in late May and early June during lambing season to eat the mineral-laden dirt. Not all of them head back up to the high country; many summer on the flanks of Bighorn Mountain, frequently crossing the road to enjoy these ponds. Because of this activity, the road may be closed for a few minutes occasionally to let the sheep cross.

A glimpse up Fall River Valley illustrates the curving "U" shape that glaciers leave behind. On the south wall of the valley, look for the ribbon of Trail Ridge Road tracing toward Many Parks Curve.

Aspenglen Campground

The smallest of the campgrounds that allows RVs, Aspenglen rests among whispering Douglas fir and pines and boasts level sites along Fall River.

Fall River Entrance Station

This structure was moved here from a location beyond Sheep Lakes. The buildings were disassembled log by log and recrafted here.

Moraine Park

The turnoff for Bear Lake lies hardly 1.5 miles west of Park Headquarters. Here, the road drops south, heading through a stand of whispering aspen trees as it rolls around the end of an immense lateral moraine. Besides being one of the best bits of acreage in Rocky to spy mule deer, the road winds through stunning Moraine Park on its way toward Bear Lake.

Moraine Park was forged 20,000 years ago, when the Thompson Glacier worked its way out of the Front Range. As it moved east, it cast aside tons of earth to the north and south,

Beavers

Beavers are the furry critters that first attracted easterners to the Rocky Mountain National Park area. Trappers explored these valleys for decades, trapping these industrious workers valued for their fur. Before the fad passed, beaver had been almost wiped out in the West.

Luckily they survived the onslaught, so we can enjoy their labors today. During summer, beavers either maintain existing wooden dams or build new ones. Many other species in the water and along the shore are dependent on the beaver's work for their survival. During the winter, beavers eat aspen and other woods they have cut and stored below the water line. They use a lot of aspen for building dams, but also build with willow and birch.

Mating for life, beavers live in dome-like houses constructed of logs and debris that are often located in the middle of a lake. They build the door under the waterline to protect themselves from predators. This helps safeguard their litters as well. Their young are born wide-eyed with two or three brothers or sisters at a time. They follow the parents around for about two years, then go off to build a dam of their own.

Moraine Park Museum

forming the two high ridges that define this valley today. Curling through the park, the Big Thompson River feeds a lively riparian habitat. Occasionally, it curls itself so tight that it cuts itself off and an oxbow lake evolves.

Moraine Park was one of the first areas settled and with plenty of water and spectacular views, it's easy to see why. In fact, at the base of the southern lateral moraine, a cluster of cabins still stands. These "in-holdings" are privately owned summer homes that have been passed down since before the park was formed. The park administration purchases these as they become available, but it's easy to see why the owners seldom sell.

Moraine Park Museum

For years, this "park" of flowers and grass has been a must-see destination for travelers. If you had arrived here in the early 1920s, you might have booked a room at the Moraine Lodge. The building that houses the museum nowadays would have been the social hall, alive with daily events. The owner and developer, Imogene McPherson, homesteaded here in 1899 and kept adding to her lodge until she died in 1928.

The Moraine Park Museum is the best museum in Rocky Mountain National Park. The building itself was constructed in the best Colorado mountain style, with dark wooden logs supporting steep gabled roofs. A stone chimney anchors one end. The first floor has a lounge facing a fireplace with a timber mantle that is covered with antlers. Near the lounge is a gallery with works of art inspired by the park.

Upstairs, under an exposed log ceiling, up-to-date exhibits explain many of the natural wonders of Rocky Mountain National Park. They answer questions many visitors ask, such as: Why are there mountains here? How does a glacier move? What is a moraine? Why so many thunderstorms? How do people affect the land? These questions are answered with displays crafted by the Denver Museum of Natural History. For some foot relief, a sitting room looks up into Moraine Park valley with a terrific view of Longs Peak and its neighbors.

The south lateral moraine—a north-facing slope—is tightly blanketed with Douglas fir, a species that thrives on little sun and much moisture. The moraine on the north—a south-facing slope— is abloom with the irregularly

Rocky As It Once Was

Bill Butler has been digging into Rocky's past. Butler, the park's archaeologist, has only been able to survey 10 of the park's 415 square miles, and already he has found 120 prehistoric or historic sites. Butler believes there are many more.

Already documented are several sites of interest. Four "game drives" have been discovered, where ancient people captured elk or deer. Another four spots show evidence of having been used for "vision quests," a Native American spiritual exercise. Several teepee sites are scattered around the park as well.

Butler uses up-to-date technology to study the past. One of Butler's favorite tools for locating sites is a remote controlled model airplane with a camera.

shaped and dispersed Ponderosa pine. These two life systems perfectly illustrate nature adjusting its species to slightly different climates: The north moraine faces the sun, so it's warmer and doesn't hold water in the ground as long; the south moraine receives much less sunshine year-round, so it's moister and cooler.

Outside the building, a half-mile nature trail winds through the Ponderosa pines behind and above the building. Trailside exhibits use the grand vistas available to discuss geology, climate, flora and fauna.

Greenback Cutthroat Trout

Here's an ecological success story. In 1973, the greenback cutthroat trout swam onto the endangered species list. Common in Colorado when Anglo-Americans first started settling this area, it was over-fished by man and out-competed by hearty, introduced trout such as the brown, rainbow and brook varieties.

Luckily, a group of cutthroat was thriving in Como Creek south of Rocky and several were transported into Hidden Valley Creek. They flourished. In 1975, all the non-native trout were removed from Bear Lake and cutthroat were released there as well. Again, success. In 1976, with a bit of fanfare, the greenback left the endangered list to the less alarming threatened list. Today, they may be found in many lakes and streams—particularly higher-elevation ones—throughout the park.

Oddly, many trout species have green backs, so no one knows how this particular one got the moniker "greenback." The cutthroat is easier to explain: each fish has a splash of bright-red coloring highlighting its lower jaw.

To spot a greenback, head for the boardwalks at the Beaver Ponds area on Trail Ridge Road. The trick is to stand very still when overlooking the water and to let them reveal themselves.

Junior Rangers

Children visiting Rocky Mountain National Park may participate in a special Junior Ranger Program. All they have to do is pick up a Junior Ranger Log Book at any of the park's visitor centers or museums.

The 26-page booklet outlines several activities such as attending a ranger-led nature walk (children must be accompanied by an adult), picking up trash, reading about safety concerns, talking to others about not feeding the wildlife and identifying any one of the four ecosystems found in Rocky Mountain National Park. One of the favorite activities is to sit quietly in one area and study only a small parcel of land at close range, counting bugs, plants and looking for animal evidence.

After kids have filled out their books as much as they can, they chat with any ranger, the ranger signs their book and presents them with a Junior Ranger badge.

Longs Peak

Mule Deer

Few visitors to Rocky Mountain National Park leave without spying at least one mule deer. These large-eared, white-rumped mammals thrive in most of the environments found here. On nearly any twilight evening, a drive from Park Headquarters south to Bear Lake will almost certainly reveal a deer or two. They are common in the Fall River cirque below the Alpine Visitor Center as well.

Averaging approximately 200 pounds, bucks keep to themselves except during the rutting season in the fall. Their antlers grow throughout the summer, and older bucks grow multi-branched racks which fall off during winter. Females live in loosely organized groups tending their young, which are born one or two at a time in the spring.

Part of the reason deer live throughout the park is because their diet is so varied. Although they have favorites such as bitterbush, they'll eat almost anything green and succulent. In winter, when foraging is more difficult, deer will even dine on the bark of aspen trees—look for scarred trunks. Mule deer munch morning and evening throughout the summer, preparing for as much as a 20 percent weight loss in the winter.

following pages: Bear Lake

Bear Lake

Moraine Park Campground/Cub Lake Trailhead/ Fern Lake Trailhead

A gravel road across from the museum leads up-valley to the Moraine Park Campground. The largest campground in the park is a surprisingly lovely spot with level sites that lie among the Ponderosa pine and overlook the valley.

Cub Lake Trailhead is the jumping-off point for a moderate five-mile round-trip hike with a 540-foot elevation gain. This hike is a favorite because it leads hikers through so many different experiences: beaver ponds, wetland habitat near the rushing water, a bit of bouldering for children and a lily-carpeted lake as the final reward.

Fern Lake Trail is considered an easy three-mile round trip with little elevation gain. Here, gargantuan boulders arch across the trail. A short hike leads on to The Pool; a lovely, calm pool surrounded by the torrents of the Big Thompson River.

Big Thompson Pullout

A third of a mile south of the museum is a pullout near the Big Thompson River. This is an excellent chance to get close to the river itself and observe wildflowers in June and July.

Bear Lake Road/ Glacier Basin

Second only to Trail Ridge Road in popularity, Bear Lake is a dream come true for day-hikers of all abilities. The lake lies jewel-like in a carved basin surrounded by perfumed woods, exalted peaks and endless Colorado sky.

The breathtaking beauty of

Autumn Pleasures

Many folks come to Rocky in September for two reasons; to see the gold of the aspen and to see and hear the elk during mating season. Here are some places you're likely to find both.

ASPEN
• The mountains all along the Peak to Peak Scenic and Historic Byway from Central City to Estes Park are often dripping in gold.
• There are many extensive aspen stands on the Bear Lake Road.
• Drive along the Kawuneeche Valley on the west side.

ELK
• The Fall River cirque below the Alpine Visitor Center.
• The meadows of Horseshoe Park, Moraine Park and Upper Beaver Meadows are all good bets.
• Best viewing is morning and evening.

the setting and the sweet serenity this spot engenders calls out to many. Trails in this cranny of the park take walkers and hikers around lakes teeming with ducks and fish, past splashing waterfalls and along vista-vivid switchbacks with aspen framing two-mile-high mountains—and those are just the easy hikes.

So many visitors to Rocky Mountain National Park find the Bear Lake basin irresistible that the lake and the surrounding areas practically choke with wilderness-worshippers nearly every summer day. Consequently, visiting in the morning before 10 a.m. or in the evening after 4 p.m. is strongly recommended. The chances of spotting wildlife and the light for photographing are actually better in these early and late hours.

Glacier Basin Campground

It has to be said that this large campground offers the most splendid view of any of the five campgrounds in Rocky. A large meadow, aflame with wildflowers much of the summer, overlooks the entire Longs Peak complex of mountains.

Shuttle Parking Lot

To relieve the congestion at Bear Lake, a parking lot has been constructed among the trees across Bear Lake Road from Glacier Basin Campground. Large, free shuttle buses make passenger pickups every half-hour or less in a loop that includes the parking lot itself, the Bierstadt Lake trailhead, Glacier Gorge Junction and Bear Lake.

Sprague Lake

Abner Sprague was one of the original homesteaders in this area. For years, he ran a hotel in Moraine Park and then sold it to build a fishing preserve.

Albert Bierstadt's *Estes Park*

At a recent showing of Bierstadt's large (five by eight feet) painting, *Estes Park,* viewers were encouraged to stand back 30 feet and study the immense canvas through binoculars. Bierstadt's attention to detail is so accurate—and extraordinary—that observers found themselves experiencing the cloud-dappled peaks and Ponderosa pine as if they were inside the landscape. Bierstadt created the work for the fourth earl of Dunraven, staying in Estes Park late in 1876 to study the vistas. The image took nearly a year to paint. Bierstadt's fee? $15,000. *Estes Park* was exhibited at London's Royal Academy before traveling to Dunraven's castle in Ireland. Today, it's the centerpiece of the Denver Public Library's Western History Department.

A mountain near Idaho Springs bears Bierstadt's name, as do a lake and a moraine in Rocky Mountain National Park.

Nowadays, a horseback riding outfitter—Glacier Creek Stables—saddles up several times a day and heads into the backcountry.

The half-mile walk along the level path that dances around Sprague Lake provides access to views of Glacier Basin itself. The high-mountain cirques are the focus of the vistas here. Blue Steller's jays, squirrels, Clark's nutcrackers and other wildlife make this lake a real nature experience, especially for children.

The Sprague Lake area is well-sprinkled with picnic tables and generous boulders to spread a blanket across for a wilderness meal.

About a third of the way around the lake, a spur trail leads off to the Sprague Lake Handicamp area. This is a fully accessible group campground for physically challenged park visitors. Reservations are required; call 970-586-1242.

Bierstadt Lake Trailhead

This trail rises about 600 feet, coursing to and fro alongside the moraine of the ancient Bierstadt Glacier. The climb dishes up rich rewards; mountain and valley views are framed exquisitely by the vertical trunks of quaking aspen. The trail peaks atop the moraine, then heads into a shady grove of lodgepole pine until it comes upon the pristine Bierstadt lake.

Glacier Gorge Trailhead

Glacier Gorge marks the start for half a dozen spectacular hikes. Most fall into the moderate to strenuous category, but the walk to Alberta Falls rises only 160 feet to meet the icy

Aspen stand

snowmelt cascading off immense granite boulders.

Bear Lake

Quite simply, Bear Lake is the jewel in the Rocky crown. Beautifully situated, it is easy to reach by car or shuttle, a joy to saunter around and most importantly, it's a delight to the eyes.

The Park Service outdid itself when it laid out the approach; it's as if a brilliant landscape architect designed it. Unfortunately, it starts with a large parking lot that is always clotted with traffic. But then, there's a ranger at a kiosk to point you toward the water tap or the trailhead bathroom. Next, you cross a wooden bridge over a stream and continue into a deep, dark wood. Just when you begin to wonder if you've lost your way, you get a glimpse of water and a glint of sunshine and, as you walk up to the overlook, Hallett Peak reveals itself, rising up 3,200 feet above the lake's surface.

The dramatic entrance is further enhanced by the half-

mile walk around the water. This trail dips and weaves among the boulders and subalpine fir forest. On the north shore, a bench invites the gaze toward Longs Peak, the Keyboard of the Winds and Pagoda Peak, which come into view. From the west end, the lake itself forms the best vista; perhaps a greenback cutthroat trout will take a fly out of the air or a Clark's nutcracker breeze by overhead.

Most of the hikes that trace trails beyond Bear Lake are moderate or strenuous. Nymph Lake and Dream Lake, both considered moderate hikes, garner fervid fans. Nymph Lake sits pretty as a postcard with its clutch of ducks and floating lily pads. The trail to Dream Lake, just beyond, rises past wildflowers, aspen and views of Bear Lake and Longs Peak before arriving at the narrow Dream Lake itself. It reflects Hallett in much the way Nymph and Bear lakes do.

Lily Lake

The Peak to Peak Scenic and Historic Highway

Not all the eastern regions of Rocky Mountain National Park are reached from inside the park itself; some are accessed from Colorado Highway 7. Because of its scenery and history, the stretch of road from Estes Park to Central City, 55 miles south, has been designated a scenic and historic byway.

Wild Basin Trailhead

The southernmost trailhead into Rocky features wild and scenic country in valleys that were shaped and re-shaped by sedimentary layering, upheaval and glaciers.

A dozen trails weave among the splendor; two are considered easy. Copeland Falls Trail follows St. Vrain Creek to a modest waterfall banked with house-size boulders. Stay on the path to play along the creek up to Calypso Cascades, a tall bank of rocks that creates

dozens of small waterfalls.

Longs Peak Campground

The smallest campground in the park is a pleasant area that is set aside for 30 tents. No recreational vehicles are allowed. This camp wakes up early with hikers headed for the Longs Peak summit.

Longs Peak Trailhead

Nearly every summer day (and many warm winter ones) hundreds of people lace up their boots, shuffle into backpacks laden with water, food and supplies and trek out to conquer Longs Peak. If not the most difficult climb in the state, it is certainly one of the most scenic. Hearty intermediate hikers will get a kick out of Chasm Lake, the gorgeous pool at the base of Longs Peak's eastern face.

Lily Lake

Isabella Bird, the English writer who passed through here in 1873, called this the "Lake of

the Lilies." At that time, the water level was lower and the lake was filled with floating lilies.

The lake is framed by Lily Mountain, Twin Sisters Mountain and the east side of Estes Cone. Located so close to Estes Park, the nature trail makes for a pleasant evening stroll.

Lily Lake Visitor Center

Rocky's newest visitor center occupies a handsome stone cabin that once housed real estate offices. Now it's home to a book shop, fireplace and helpful rangers. Great displays exhibit useful information on winter use, hiking, wildflowers, birdwatching, wildlife and local history. The center also dispenses material on the nearby Roosevelt and Arapaho National Forests. Another display explains what the differences are between these governmental entities.

The Roof of the Rockies

Trail Ridge Road

H ere unfurls the top of the world, the roof of the Rockies, the apex of America. Scalloped massifs climb from verdant valleys to ridges and pinnacles of bare stone that appear like granite jaws gnashing at thunder, wind and rain. Eons ago, massive ice fields gouged-out valleys and sterling, glacial lakes as easily as a baker stamps biscuits out of dough. Atop the rocky ridge's highest escarpment, the Continental Divide separates the watersheds of the Atlantic and Pacific oceans—both of which are hundreds of miles away.

Not all is naked rock: Tufted carpets of ancient tundra roll like emerald meadows under the so-close sky. Here, elk graze on flora no wider or taller than a hand but with roots nearly as deep as a tree.

Across these highlands, the wind rarely stops blowing—it may wail past at more than a hundred miles per hour or whisper by as a fragrant breeze. Snow may fill up nooks and crannies 25 feet deep. Lightning strikes are as common here as ground squirrels in the forest below.

Yet this tundra is hospitable to abundant wildlife. Elk summer here. Yellow-bellied marmots and picas scurry among the rock formations. Eagles and hawks rise effortlessly on the breeze to espy their dinner.

Humans come to feel the bite of the wind themselves as they shake their heads in awe at this panorama of mountain peaks; to admire a bull elk and his harem; to have their breath stolen by the beauty of a flower no bigger than a fingernail; to drive at 12,000 feet above sea level along the top of the world.

Trail Ridge Road

Trail Ridge Road is the definitive scenic drive in Rocky Mountain National Park—perhaps in all of Colorado. Open only from mid-May to mid-October, the highest continuously paved road in the nation rolls west from Deer Ridge

left: Alpine tundra along Trail Ridge Road

Junction, then angles south at the Alpine Visitor Center to drop into the Kawuneeche Valley—the headwaters of the Grand-Canyon-carving Colorado River—before reaching Grand Lake, Colorado.

While it may only traverse 39 miles horizontally, it ascends (and descends) several thousand feet vertically, climbing 3,246 feet from Deer Ridge Junction on the east to reach a high spot near the Alpine Visitor Center, then dropping 3,500 feet into Grand Lake, Colorado. If those heights were office buildings, one would be 360 stories high and the other, 390.

Along the course, Trail Ridge rolls through every habitat existent in the park: riparian, montane, subalpine and alpine. Often, it traipses past herds of elk and other wild things but it always advances through panoramic views. In fact, one way to think of Trail Ridge Road is as a two-lane, paved nature trail.

History of Trail Ridge Road

Native Americans have been traversing these same valleys and cresting these same hillocks for thousands of years. In fact, the term modern users coined for the road—Trail Ridge—honors the Ute whose "trail" along the tundra's "ridge" we still follow. Ute and Arapaho walked this and many other trails in the park to travel from the high mountains to lower elevations, where bison were once abundant. Because the tundra heals so slowly, the ancient paths they took are still visible in many places along the modern highway.

Alpine Tundra Ecosystem

Elevation: Above 11,500 feet
Description: A dense mat of low-lying vegetation characterizes the alpine tundra. Few plants achieve much height because of the severe climate, yet the area is vibrant with easily observable wildlife. Almost one-third of Rocky is above timberline, making it one of the largest expanses of tundra in the lower 48 states. So delicate is this area that a trampled patch may take 400 to 1,000 years to recover.
Microclimate: Constant wind gusts occasionally to 170 mph; temperatures range from a brisk -30° Fahrenheit to a barely-warm 65° Fahrenheit; it has a growing season of only 45 days; there is intense ultraviolet radiation; there are frequent afternoon thunderstorms.
Tree types: At the upper limit of the treeline, some fir and spruce trees survive in a stunted, windblown form called krummholz.
Where to go: Trail Ridge Road from approximately one mile west of Rainbow Curve to well west of Medicine Bow Curve rolls atop the alpine tundra. The Tundra Trailhead at Rock Cut has a paved walkway leading into the tundra that is lined with illustrative panels. Dress warmly and wear wind gear.
Undergrowth types: Chiming bells and rosy paintbrush often grow alongside dwarfed willow bushes.
Animal types: Elk, bighorn sheep, mule deer, yellow-bellied marmot, pika, white-tailed ptarmigan.
Wildflowers: Alpine avens, blue harebells, fairy primroses, yellow-marsh marigolds and many others form a thick mat of plants. The longer you look at any area, the more species you pick out.

Subalpine Ecosystem

Elevation: 9,500 to 11,500 (treeline)
Description: Closely spaced, moisture-loving trees form a band that extends from damp valley floors to the treeline.
Microclimate: Snow blown in from the tundra by the constant winds make subalpine ecosystems among the wettest parts of the park. Snow may not melt here until midsummer.
Tree Types: Engelmann spruce and subalpine fir dominate; aspen and lodgepole pine fill in damaged areas. At treeline, the constant wind and pressure from snow shapes trees so that they only have leaves and branches on their downwind side; such trees are called krummholz.
Where to Go: Trail Ridge Road from Many Parks Curve to Rainbow Curve is in the subalpine zone, as is Bear Lake and the simpler hikes thereabouts.
Undergrowth Types: Common juniper, Colorado currant, wild raspberry.
Animal Types: Snowshoe hare, least chipmunk, red squirrel, mountain chickadee, pine grosbeak. Elk and deer graze the lower elevations.
Wildflowers: Jacob's ladder, columbine, woodnymph, golden banner.

Hidden Valley

Driving The High Country

Trail Ridge Road loops high into the alpine tundra, rising some 4,200 feet between Estes Park and the Alpine Visitor Center. Here are some tips for high-altitude driving.

- Automobiles from lower elevations around the country may not perform the way they usually do. They often experience vapor lock, when the car stalls or overheats. Staying in lower gears helps. Don't pump the accelerator; it'll flood the engine.
- Top off the gas tank and air the tires. There are no service stations within the park's boundaries.
- Use lower gears—on the uphill, it will help avoid vapor lock and on the downhill, it will spare the brake pads.

- Avoid riding the brake. Gear down or tap the brakes—they can overheat easily.
- Keeping eyes on the road can often be tricky with Rocky Mountain vistas rolling by, but Trail Ridge Road is full of twists, turns and narrow shoulders that require a driver's full attention.
- Be very careful when pulling onto the roadway. Those tight curves can hide a moving car or a speeding bicyclist.
- Three reasons to travel in the morning or evening: less traffic, more wildlife, better light for photography.
- Lock the car when it is unattended.

Almost as soon as the Old Fall River Road and the western portion of Trail Ridge Road were completed in 1920, the park's superintendent, Roger Toll, began envisioning a newer, wider road that would allow visitors to experience more of the park's spectacular vistas. Special construction techniques were used because Toll was determined that the road not mar the landscape but rather fit it like a glove.

Begun in 1929 and constructed by Colorado road builder C. A. Colt, the eastern portion of Trail Ridge was opened to traffic in the summer of 1932.

Deer Ridge Junction

Deer Ridge Junction is the decision point for people heading through the park. To the west rises Trail Ridge Road and to the north lie Horseshoe Park and Old Fall River Road— the one-way gravel road that follows Fall River. Both top out at the Alpine Visitor Center.

This juncture was once the location of a congested group of hotels, restaurants and gift shops. In the 1960s, the park purchased the land from the Schubert family (who had developed it), removed the old structures and re-planted the area. Today, barely a trace survives of all those buildings—a testimonial to the heartiness of the Ponderosa parkland habitat at this elevation.

Heading west up Trail Ridge Road, look for a lateral moraine deposited here 20,000 years ago by the Fall River Glacier. This moraine looks like a tall ridge running parallel to the valley and is thick with lodgepole pine, Ponderosa pine and Douglas fir. Chewed-off aspen stumps are evidence that beavers often dined here.

Beaver Ponds

The boardwalk at this pull-off paves an easy trail to the handiwork of a beaver family that has been working on Hidden Valley Creek since the 1950s.

Beavers are industrious builders, constructing dams on creeks to raise water levels, which form ponds. Pools provide a safe haven for these large rodents as they build their houses in these small lakes, with the entrance below the water line. Aspen and willow trees are the staple diet of beavers. Adults prefer bark and new growth wood while younger animals enjoy leaves and branches.

These ponds support many other species as well. The threatened greenback cutthroat trout thrives here, feeding on insects. Belted kingfisher and other birds in turn feed on the fish. Coyotes are common in the meadows, as are mice, deer and elk. In cold weather, porcupines winter in the branches of trees.

Longs Peak

By the time Major Stephen H. Long's expedition sighted the mountain that would one day bear his name, Native Americans had been using it as a landmark for generations. One story tells how they climbed to its top to build eagle blinds; they captured the feathered foragers, plucked a few tail feathers and set them free.

Of course, even before the Native Americans used Longs Peak, it had reposed there for eons, its hooked nose sniffing at the wind, its bright face glittering toward the great Eastern Plains. It pushed itself out of the ground between 50 and 70 million years ago from rock laid down as far back in time as 1.4 billion years ago.

Then the glacial work began. Glaciers flowed and melted here many times. The peak and faces we see today owe much to frozen rivers, which were at their thickest about 20,000 years ago.

Today, we enjoy the 14,255-foot peak—not even among Colorado's top ten—from throughout the park and from all along the Front Range. Hundreds of climbers attempt its flanks every year.

Women on Longs Peak

Not much is known about Addie Alexander except newspaper reports that list her as the first woman to scale Longs Peak. That report was run on August 26, 1871, and that's the last that was heard of Addie Alexander.

Anna Dickinson, an early women's rights advocate, was the second. She spent the summer of 1873 topping "14ers"— Pikes Peak, Mount Lincoln, Grays Peak. Dickinson was probably the first woman to crest Mount Elbert, Colorado's highest. On September 13, 1873, she and several men from the Hayden Survey who were surveying the Rockies ascended Longs Peak. Much to the dismay of the men she was with, Dickinson wore pants for the climb—an almost unforgivable *faux pas* for the time.

Perhaps the most interesting of the early Longs Peak climbers, Isabella Bird, was an English writer who came to Colorado for an extended visit. Determined to get to the top of Longs because she thought it so beautiful, she hired a local—and notorious— mountain man, Mountain Jim, to guide her. Unfortunately, Bird was not in top physical condition and Jim literally carried her "like a bale of goods" to the top. Isabella wrote her sister long letters about her adventures which, after editing out certain scandalous passages about Jim, became the book, *A Lady's Life in the Rocky Mountains*.

Alpenglow on east face of Longs Peak

Hidden Valley

An ecologist driving through the aspen and lodgepole pine near this deserted ski area might comment that there had been a forest fire recently. Indeed, a fire did rage through here. In 1915, there was still logging going on at this end of the valley. One night, a ranger who had been stationed to watch a smoldering sawdust pile snuck off to see his girl-friend in Estes Park. The fire that sprang from the pile ripped through the mature Engelmann spruce and subalpine fir forest.

The lodgepole pine and aspen that forest the mountain now between Hidden Valley and Many Parks Curve are two species that grow easily into areas opened up by natural disasters such as fires or avalanches—that's how the ecologist would know. Chances are good that the spruce and fir will return eventually as the cool, wet sub-climate in this "hidden" valley are perfect for them.

Many Parks Curve

Many Parks Curve is one of the most dramatic stops on Trail Ridge Road. Approaching from either direction, you can actually drive past the boardwalk overlook to a parking lot that enables you to turn right—instead of across traffic—to get off the road.

When most people think of parks, they either think of manicured, grassy areas in towns or national landmarks like Yosemite or Yellowstone National Park. Here, though,

Lawn Lake Flood

Looking toward Horseshoe Park from either Many Parks Curve or Rainbow Curve brings into view a broad triangle of rocks as the valley floor edges up the lateral moraine near Bighorn Mountain. This is the debris left when the Lawn Lake dam broke.

The dam burst on July 15, 1982, at 5:30 in the morning. Luckily, a park employee was in the area and called downstream with a warning. Still, the torrent brought 18,000 cubic feet of water per second crashing down into the valley.

It was carrying a lot of rock—364,000 cubic yards of debris, enough to cover the 42 acres visible. The flood inflicted serious damage to Estes Park and killed three campers.

Off to a Rocky Start

15,000 to 10,000 B.C.: Evidence—arrows, knives and spears—puts humans in the park some 10,000 years ago. What these Clovis and Folsom points don't tell us is what these early hunters were doing. Were they stalking game or merely passing through?

6,000 B.C. to 500 A.D.: Humans in this period construct rock-wall structures to funnel deer and elk into the waiting weapons of hunters. Several of these "game drives" exist in Rocky Mountain National Park. It's also probable that these people gathered berries to round out their diet.

500 to 1600 A.D.: Ancient people begin to develop into the "tribes" we are familiar with today. The Ute cross through the area once or twice a year, following the migratory patterns of animals.

1600: When the Ute obtain horses, bison become their primary food and they trot through the area frequently in search of them.

Mid-1700s: The Ute find themselves in conflict with the Comanche and Arapaho.

1800: The Arapaho dominate the region, having moved south from regions to the north. Their trails across the tundra are still in use today.

1846: Trapper Rufus B. Sage publishes the tales of his adventures, *Rocky Mountain Life, or Startling Scenes and Perilous Adventures in the Far West during an Expedition of Three Years.* The particular beauty of the area seems to appeal to trappers.

1859: Gold is discovered in Colorado and the boom is on. Joel Estes arrives hoping to strike it

Historic photo of the Stanley Hotel

rich but finds greater stability in cattle ranching, supplying elk and bighorn sheep to Denver butchers and renting rooms to vistaviewers.

1864: William Byers, editor and owner of Denver's *Rocky Mountain News*, attempts to climb Longs Peak. His trip is a failure but his stories about the area generate interest.

1868: Byers and western explorer extraordinaire John Wesley Powell attain the top of Longs Peak. Byer's tales continue to raise interest in the region and nationally.

1873: English author Isabella Bird spends the autumn exploring the area. She attempts to climb Longs Peak but her guide—"Mountain" Jim Nugent—actually carries her part of the way. Bird's letters to her sister become a popular book: *A Lady's Life in the Rocky Mountains.*

1873: The Fourth Earl of Dunraven returns after an 1872 trip to begin buying land. Eventually, employing questionable

methods, he assembles virtual control of more than 15,000 acres. Immediately, ranchers such as Abner Sprague and Alexander MacGregor contest Dunraven's land acquisition but the Earl's inn does well, bringing many tourists. Eventually, the pressure becomes too great and Dunraven abandons the region.

Mid-1870s to early 1880s: Gold discoveries along the Upper Colorado River bring thousands of miners to the western slopes. Lucky for visitors today, few minerals are abundant here and the miners moved on, leaving the area with little evidence of mining.

1881 to 1936: Construction of the Grand Ditch water diversion project begins on the upper reaches of the Never Summer Range. This canal—eight to 20 feet wide and more than 14 miles long—carries water from the upper third of the mountains to a tunnel and eventually, to farms on the Eastern Plains.

1905: The acreage between

Off to a Rocky Start

Mt. Chapin

Estes Park and Grand Lake becomes part of the Medicine Bow Forest Preserve. However, not much changes; forestry continues, as does cattle ranching and mining.

1907: F.O. Stanley, the wealthy co-inventor of photographic processes and a steam-driven automobile, begins construction of the Stanley Hotel.

1909: Dissatisfaction with the ongoing uses of the region prompts people to propose a national park. Though some landowners disagree, regional, state and federal officials such as President Theodore Roosevelt believe the idea has merit.

Enos Mills, local inn owner, tour guide and naturalist, begins the campaign to gain national park status for Rocky. Though he originally envisioned a much larger park extending from Estes Park to Colorado Springs, he accepts a reduction in size. Mills is a good speaker and excellent writer. His many books, as well as articles in magazines such as the *Saturday*

Evening Post, Harper's and *Atlantic,* effectively spread the word about how special the vales and peaks between Estes and Grand Lake really are.

1915: On January 26, President Woodrow Wilson signs the bill to create Rocky Mountain National Park. At this time, much of the land in the eastern parks, such as Moraine and Horseshoe, is dotted with ranches and no trails or visitor centers exist.

1913 to 1920: Convict labor constructs the Fall River Road, linking the eastern and western portions of the park for the first time.

1920s: Almost 250,000 people visit Rocky the first year that the Fall River Road is completed (1920). Throughout the 1920s, campsites, trails, nature programs and recreational activities are developed.

1926 to 1933: The dream of Park Superintendent Roger W. Toll becomes reality as Trail Ridge Road nears completion. Toll believes in parks as sanctuaries and that visitors should be provided with

easy access to the park's greatest bounty—its alpine tundra.

1940 to the mid-1950s: The Colorado-Big Thompson water diversion project is constructed. This massive water project, begun under the presidency of Franklin Roosevelt, creates two enormous lakes on the western slope—Shadow Mountain Reservoir and Lake Granby—as well as the Alva B. Adams tunnel, a 13.1-mile-long underground waterway shuttling 550 cubic feet of water per second from the Western Slope to the Eastern Plains.

1950s to the present: Significant "cleaning up" of the park has taken place in the last several decades: privately held land has been purchased, old buildings removed and damaged landscape revegetated. In addition, many new trails have been cut, visitor centers and museums added and programs developed with the needs of the park's many visitors in mind.

the word indicates a large, level, grassy area surrounded by mountains. In this case, the parks visible from the walkway were gouged out of V-shaped valleys by a slab of ice hundreds of feet thick and eight miles long. When this wedge melted 13,000 to 14,000 years ago, it left behind the masses of stone, silt and gravel it had gathered on its way.

From the vantage point of the wooden walkway, you can spot Beaver Meadows in the foreground. The dark green, evergreen-covered ridge is a moraine of earth pushed aside by the glacier. Beyond lies Moraine Park. The river winding its way through the park is the Big Thompson. Next lies another fir-cloaked moraine and farther south rise many mountains of the Front Range: Longs Peak, Chiefs Head Peak, Thatchtop, Taylor and Hallett Peaks. From the lower end of the lower parking lot, observe Horseshoe Park as well as portions of Hondius and Estes Parks—hence the name, Many Parks Curve.

The craggy knob of rock jutting out of the lower parking lot itself is made up of biotite schist, Silver Plume granite and pegmatite—rocks that individually make up much of the rock in Rocky. At this site, they are blended together by complex geological processes.

Upper Hidden Valley

Look to the north while skirting along Upper Hidden Valley; high above climbs Trail Ridge Road as it banks around Rainbow Curve. This is one of Trail Ridge Road's steepest stretches.

This length of road runs through the heart of a classic subalpine ecosystem. Cool due to sun patterns and wet due to snow conditions, these forests are thick with Engelmann spruce, subalpine fir and limber pine. Dense tree patches, struggling for light and warmth in the short growing season, prevent sun from reaching the forest floor. Deer and elk are found here but more common are smaller mammals. Patient wildlife watchers might spot porcupines, martens and shrews.

Birds such as great horned owls and hawks are plentiful.

Drive into the pullout on the north side of the road and look up-slope to see water tumbling precipitously down a small channel in the rock. This is one of the most popular photography spots on Trail Ridge Road as it's the only permanent waterfall. Be very mindful of cars and bicycles if you cross the road.

Two-mile Marker

Not far beyond Upper Hidden Valley, Trail Ridge Road

Rocky's Historian

Combine the terms "Rocky Mountain National Park" and "history," and it doesn't take long to turn up Curt Buchholtz. After all, Buchholtz wrote the 255-page classic *Rocky Mountain National Park: A History,* as well as much of the National Parkways guide to Rocky and the introductions to several other books.

Buchholtz came to Rocky from Glacier National Park in 1985, "I was kind of doing the freelance writer thing," says Buchholtz, "when this position came open."

"This position" is that of executive director of both the Rocky Mountain Nature Association and Rocky Mountain National Park Associates. You see, Curt doesn't just write about Rocky, he's determined to make it a better place. The associates group is a "friends-of-the-park" organization, which raises money and provides volunteer efforts to improve the park.

Recently, the Associates built the handicap accessible trail

around Lily Lake. They've also provided funds to build a greenhouse so plants are available to landscape areas trodden with traffic. And they've raised money for several visitor centers and exhibit projects.

As someone who knows much about the park's past, how does he think its future appears? "We need to strike a balance between wilderness and the large population of people along Colorado's Front Range who want to use Rocky," Buchholtz says. "We want the park to be usable by the widest possible variety of people."

Weathered tree in mountain landscape at Rainbow Curve

crosses a point exactly two miles (10,560 feet) above sea level.

Rainbow Curve

Unless it has rained recently, the name of this curve won't make much sense. If it has just stopped raining and the sun has broken through the clouds, as it does on dozens of summer afternoons, the multiple rainbows visible from this bend in the road make the name obvious.

An immense amount of Rocky Mountain National Park's acreage is visible from this lookout. To the north, you can sense the craggy tops of Mount Chapin and Ypsilon

Picnic Time

Rocky Mountain National Park has countless places to spread out a picnic. The following locales are recommended because they have tables in particularly pretty settings and plenty of space for kids to play.

Along Bear Lake Road
• Just shy of three miles south of the U.S. Highway 36 turnoff at Tuxedo Junction, look for a picnic table to the east among the pine trees. If this isn't quite scenic enough, head down the trail to a group of tables in a shady pine grove.
• Sprague Lake: East of the parking lot are many tables near a creek that often bobs with ducks.
• Prospect Canyon: Just before the odometer shows eight miles after turning south off U.S. Highway 36, look for a table perched among the trees on the edge of the cliff that skirts Prospect Canyon.

Moraine Park
• Take the road toward the Moraine Park Campground and keep your eyes peeled for a group of tables under the Ponderosa pine trees on the north (right) side of the road. These offer great views of Longs Peak and there are plenty of wildflowers to admire. Often, mule deer linger here around sunset.

Upper Beaver Meadows
• Less than a mile after you enter via the Beaver Meadows Entrance Station and drive toward Deer Ridge Junction, look for a dirt road on the west (left). Follow this dirt road to its end and find several tables adjacent to the creek at the trailhead.

Horseshoe Park
• Endovalley Picnic Site: Just before Old Fall River Road careens up the valley, a picnic area has been built among the trees and willow bushes. Many of the tables are in reasonably private settings and the Fall River itself adds background music.

Kawuneeche Valley
• Lake Irene: This setting on a picturesque alpine lake is located west of the Milner Pass/Continental Divide pullout. Be sure to take a stroll along the trail.

Mountain—the Mummy Range. The triangle of white rocks strewn on the valley floor is an alluvial fan that formed when the Lawn Lake flood of 1982 spewed out thousands of tons of rock. Between the fan and Horseshoe Park is Bighorn Mountain, home to many bighorn sheep. The middle ground reveals Deer Mountain, Lumpy Ridge, Estes Park and even the eastern plains of Colorado. To the south begins the rhythm of the Rockies: tall craggy mountains interrupted by deep forested valleys.

Yellow-bellied Marmots

When it comes to tundra begging, these critters are nearly as persistent about food as the squirrels are at lower elevations. While it is tempting to slip them a peanut, it is important for the animals' own survival that they do not get used to human food. Please do not feed them.

Indeed, yellow-bellied marmots are common in the tundra. They thrive in colonies dominated by a single male. They clear out a home for themselves by burrowing into rock piles. And they claim territory for themselves, including nearby boulders, which they use as watchtowers.

What are they looking for? Predators. The fat these rodent-relatives build up over the summer makes fine fare for eagles, coyotes and bobcats. If you hear

a high-pitched squeal drift in on the wind, it's probably because a yellow-bellied marmot noticed you and it's warning its neighbors.

Yellow-bellied marmots need all those extra pounds because they hibernate in their nests during the frigid winters from October to March. Soon after they wake up, they bear three to six blind, hairless babies.

The Continental Divide from Trail Ridge Road

Knife-edge

Approximately half a mile west of Rainbow Curve, the edges of the road drop away into valleys on both sides. Drivers always seem to slow at this magical point, sensing the immensity of Hidden Valley to the south and Hanging Valley to the north.

A hanging valley is formed when a smaller glacier flows into a larger one, the way a creek flows into a river. Here, Hanging Valley "flows" into the Fall River Valley.

The big bite out of Sundance Mountain is a cirque, the area where a glacier starts. As the glacier builds up over time, the places where the ice touches the mountain freeze and thaw many times. This breaks off rocks over many years and the bowl carves itself out.

This area—called tree limit or timberline—is the transition zone between the subalpine forest and the tundra itself. The elevation at timberline in Colorado is roughly 11,500 feet above sea level.

What appear to be shrubs in this area are really trees. These "tree islands" start in the wind shadow of a boulder or rock outcropping and gradually spread, literally moving across the tundra landscape as their branches touch the ground and take root. Many of these tree islands are more than a thousand years old.

Windblown trees called banner trees or krummholz have leaves only on one side. This results from the wind shearing off leaves and branches on the windy side. While they may not look very large or aged, many of them are hundreds of years old. If they were in a more hospitable climate—perhaps at Hidden Valley only a few yards away—they would be much larger.

Ute Crossing

A small turnout on the south with a display sign marks one of the spots where the old Ute trail crosses Trail Ridge Road. These ancient footpaths were traversed up to 11,000 years ago.

People back then built low rock walls to funnel game into traps. From these heights, they also built blinds to capture eagles for their feathers.

Forest Canyon Overlook

A short walk on an asphalt trail leads nature lovers through an alpine wilderness to a fenced overlook. The Big Thompson Canyon itself falls away thousands of feet down to the river, barely visible and snaking through the trees below. The river cut a deep valley here along a crack in the earth's crust. Glaciers, beginning in the mountains across from the overlook, carved the valley into the smooth dipped-out shape we see today.

Across the valley is a sampler of many glacial effects. The big quarter-dome bites are immense cirques—the circular starting points of glacial activities. Along the top edges run arêtes, carved out on two sides. Pinnacles have been carved on several sides. Hanging lakes or tarns form as the

glacier digs huge holes below the ice. Hanging valleys form where a small glacier flows into a larger one.

Keep an eye on the tundra; elk seem to gather along the two-mile stretch from the

Survival of the Fittest

Question: With temperatures that dip below -50° Fahrenheit and winds that regularly howl faster than 100 MPH, how can plants survive in the tundra? Answer: Specialized adaptations.

Moss campion survives the wind and cold because of its low, compact shape, which traps heat and moisture in dense, mat-like leaves.

Whiplash saxifrage reproduces by runners rather than seeds. Runners continue to live, while seeds might not have time to sprout and mature in the short growing season. On the other hand, Koenigia is believed to be the only annual in the tundra that can burst into bloom, be pollinated and produce seeds in five weeks.

Plant hairs, like those on Rydbergia, help reduce heat loss and trap heat.

The ground-hugging rosette leaves of the snowball saxifrage stay below the level of the drying wind. While the wind at human-head level may be 30 to 50 mph, it may be much slower at ground level.

Some plants develop special roots. The big-rooted spring beauty may be only a hand-sized plant, but its taproot may sink up to five feet into the thick tundra soil.

overlook to Rock Cut.

Rock Cut

Rock Cut, one of the most fascinating turn-offs in the park, has parking areas on both sides of the road as well as rest rooms.

A smooth, asphalt-paved trail called the Tundra World Nature Trail bee-lines from the parking lot to a rock formation a half-mile away. Though the distance may not be far, wind, cold and altitude can make a simple hike seem like hard work.

The tundra is an area of extreme climate. For five months a year, the temperature never rises above 0° Fahrenheit. It stays below the freezing point for another five months; indeed, the highest temperature ever recorded in Colorado's tundra was 63° F. There are 25 percent more ultraviolet rays here than at sea level, so the sun is much more intense. Also, the wind simply never stops blowing, raging frequently to 150 mph.

Life thrives here because the plants in the tundra are specially adapted for these conditions. Most are small and stay clumped close

to the ground where the wind is not as fierce. Many contain anthocyanin, a chemical that uses sunlight to produce heat. Hair on stems and leaves also reduce heat loss.

A visit in the morning or evening might yield a siting of the white-tailed ptarmigan that live in the rocks. These birds live here year-round, changing their plumage from a mottled summer camouflage to pure white for the winter.

Even the rocks are affected by tundra conditions. Up to a hundred freeze-thaw cycles may occur every year. This, combined with the action of the permanently frozen ground just below the surface (the permafrost), cause many unusual rock formations. Due to permafrost heave, rocks often form themselves into straight stripes, loopy garlands and even polygons.

Lava Cliffs

Two miles west of Rock Cut, Lava Cliffs come into view. As difficult as it may be to believe, these cliffs were formed by welded volcanic ash (tuff) that originated in the Never Summer Range some eight miles west. They have been etched by glaciers

Point of interest marker #6 for Rock Cut trail

left: Rock Cut; following page: Mummy Range

to take on an almost "southwest butte" appearance. The bowl at the base of this formation often contains elk.

Highest Point

About a half-mile west of Lava Cliffs, a sign celebrates the high point of Trail Ridge Road (12,183 feet above sea level), the highest paved spot in America.

Gore Range Overlook

This place provides an expansive vista of much of central Colorado. Far to the left rises Longs Peak; across the valley the dramatic peaks of the Front Range crescendo with Jackstraw Mountain; to the southwest the Gore Range dimples the horizon, just beyond lies Vail Valley; and to the right unfurl the silver and red peaks of the Never

Summer Range, which form the western edge of the park.

Alpine Visitor Center/ Fall River Pass

The Alpine Visitor Center marks the top of Fall River Pass, a route used for centuries by Native Americans, which connects the Fall River and Cache la Poudre valleys.

The immense circular bowl below is the Fall River cirque.

Elk

When Joel Estes and his family arrived, elk (also called wapiti by Native Americans) were so common that hunting them for restaurants in Denver to raise ready cash involved little more than walking outside with a gun. In fact, killing these sources of meat became so frequent that by 1880, Abner Sprague reported seeing the last one die. The entire population was decimated in 20 years.

Luckily, folks came to their senses. In 1913, 49 elk were imported from Wyoming and in the summer of 1996, Rocky supported 3,200 elk.

Wapiti are grazing animals that spend most of their lives foraging for food mornings and evenings, and napping the rest of the day. During summer they head for higher and cooler elevations, and in the winter they head down into the valleys—often right into Estes Park itself—to snack on willow, sagebrush and aspen.

Only a few predators will attack an elk. A bobcat or a group of coyotes will assault a sick adult or calf, but only a mountain lion has the courage to take on a full-

grown elk, and then only rarely.

These majestic animals can weigh from 400 to 1,000 pounds. Males lose their antler racks annually; females don't grow antlers.

Every autumn the male elk howl or "bugle" to attract harems of females. This is a favorite time to see elk in Rocky Mountain National Park. Calves are born in the spring.

Tundra Walk at Alpine Visitor Center

Dinosaur Life

While thousands of feet of ice were working their way down the valleys of Rocky during all those ice ages, the place was alive with animals.

If you woke up one morning 100,000 years ago and stepped out of your cave, you might spot saber-toothed tigers, mastodons, giant sloths, bison and wooly mammoths in the region of the park. Though most didn't make it to the modern age, the bison did—until they were nearly decimated in the 1800s.

Travel further back in time to find *Stegosaurus* lumbering about near what is now Red Rocks Park near Denver. Insects thrived a little farther south at Florrisant Fossil Beds National Monument. And dozens of Jurassic-Park-type creatures occupied the landscape west of Rocky, which eventually became Dinosaur National Monument.

The only fossils actually found in the park are the shells of some marine animals, which have been discovered in the Never Summer Range on the north side of the park.

This has been the headwall or high-mountain kick-off point for many glaciers over thousands of years. It is also one of the most dependable places to find elk in the summer and fall; scan for cinnamon-brown lumps lounging along the edges of the bushes.

The visitor center occupies two buildings, both anchored against the wind with log super-structures. A stone-railed viewing platform invites looks into the cirque and beyond to Sundance Mountain. One building contains a book store, a glass-walled overlook and a set of exhibits on the natural processes of the alpine tundra: rocks, glaciers, frost, seasonal changes, plant survival, krummholz, animal adaptations and maps. Park rangers attend an information desk. The other building houses a large gift shop and cafeteria— the only ones within Rocky Mountain National Park. There are no automobile facilities at the center.

A quarter-mile-long stairway leads to an overlook with 360° views. Deer, elk, falcons, yellow-bellied marmots and pica, often visible from this point, don't seem to mind the wind or altitude at all.

Medicine Bow Curve

This provides the best full-on view to the north end of the park. The dominant, gentle-sloped mountain across the valley is Specimen Mountain, built with layer upon layer of volcanic ash melted into stone by its own heat—tuff. In the distance, the Medicine Bow Range of Colorado rises and even farther beyond

Never Summer Range

Wyoming's Snowy Range crinkles the horizon. To the right is the Mummy Range, glimpsed earlier from Rainbow Curve.

The chasm below is the glacier-gouged valley of the Cache la Poudre River. The ice that dug this cleft accumulated from the valley floor to where the treeline now skirts the mountains' shoulders. The river basin, too wet to maintain forest, grows extensive willow and other bushes that sustain the mule deer and elk herds that fleck this trough.

A medicine bow is a tall wooden staff decorated with feathers and other amulets that Native Americans used to evoke supernatural powers. The Medicine Bow Mountains of Colorado are named after the river in Wyoming of the same name.

Commonly called the Poudre, the Cache la Poudre River got its name from French-speaking Creole trappers who hid a cache of gunpowder downstream.

Continental Divide/Milner Pass

The Continental Divide drapes across Trail Ridge Road at the Milner Pass pull-off. Here, the destiny of raindrops is decided. Droplets falling on the west of this invisible line will drip into Beaver Creek, which gurgles into the Colorado River—the river that carves the Grand Canyon floats houseboats on Lake Powell before emptying into the Gulf of California. Moisture molecules landing to the east make their way to the Cache la Poudre, roll into the South Platte and spill into the Platte River and Missouri rivers before splashing into the Mississippi and the Gulf of Mexico.

The Continental Divide

The Grand Ditch

This ditch, called Grand, isn't really grand at all—it's more of an eyesore scarring the upper reaches of the Never Summer Range. The ditch was named for the river that is now called the Colorado, but which was called the Grand River until 1921.

The Grand Ditch itself (eight to 20 feet wide and six feet deep) accumulates runoff from the streams and brooks along a 14-mile length of the Never Summers. It then transports the water to a tunnel that eventually satiates farms and cities on the arid Eastern Plains.

One of the earliest water diversion projects in the state, it was begun in 1890 and completed in 1936. Much of the early construction was done by hand with Chinese and European laborers.

Trail Ridge Road

splits the two climates in Rocky Mountain National Park as well. The western half of the park receives much more snow and rain. It battles less wind but shivers with considerably colder temperatures.

Lake Irene

Lake Irene glistens in a glade of subalpine fir, inviting park visitors to enjoy a picnic and savor a quiet walk around the water.

Farview Curve

Undoubtedly the best seat in the house for spying on the Never Summer Mountains beyond and the Kawuneeche Valley below, this pullout roosts nearly 1,000 feet above the snaking Colorado River. In the mist of the distance floats the Vasquez Range.

The Never Summers unroll to the north draped in Douglas fir, bejeweled with aspen and crowned with granite, schist and gneiss. The aptly named Red Mountain wears a mantle of iron-rich ochre stone. Along the mountains' bases dawdle the Colorado River's headwaters, lazily drifting to and fro across the perfectly formed valley floor. Moose wallow in the willow down there, as do elk and deer. Coyotes and mountain lions compete for food.

Colorado River Trailhead

The parking area on the west side of the road marks the jumping-off spot for a fascinating hike. The Colorado River Trail courses up-valley, leading to the very spring where the first drips of the mighty river form. Along the way huddle the unearthly remains of Camp Wheeler (a dude ranch run by a Colorado character named Squeaky Bob Wheeler) and Lulu City (the remains of a never-quite-struck-

it-rich mining town). Luckily for today's visitors to the park, few useful minerals were found in the mines hereabouts, so very few mine tailings mar the vistas. The hike to Lulu City, although relatively level, is 3.5 miles each way.

Timber Creek Campground

The only campground inside Rocky Mountain National Park on the western slope, this rather large campground spreads out among groves of lodgepole pine.

Never Summer Ranch

This rugged, old-style dude ranch is the destination of a half-mile stroll through the Kawuneeche Valley—an Arapaho word meaning "Valley of the Coyote"—and across the Colorado riverbed itself.

Johnny Holzwarth wrangled a dude ranch here from

103

the 1920s to the 1970s. The accommodations seem crude today but as the site interpreters point out, guests in those days came for that very ruggedness, for the fantasy of getting away from it all to hunt and fish in the wild. The guides lead tours of the log buildings several times a day during the summer. Visitors may also lead themselves using a self-guided tour booklet.

Harbison Meadow

The large parking lot looks over a treeless meadow once awash with hay planted by two sisters, Annie and Kitty Harbison, who homesteaded this tract in 1895. The sisters originally built small cabins for themselves but as their dairy business grew, they splurged on a house big enough to contain their brother, mother and father.

Kawuneeche Visitor Center

This simple wood building provides a variety of services for park guests. Rangers answer questions about the park as they consult several maps at the counter. A small book store provides printed information. A model of the park suggests possible itineraries for stays of different lengths. A film illustrates the splendor of the park and display cases

Bighorn Sheep

Rocky Mountain National Park's signature animal is the bighorn sheep. In fact, the Colorado legislature has bestowed the title of "State Mammal" on the animal's curlicue-crowned head.

Growing to about three feet high, these animals weigh in at 125 to 225 pounds, depending on whether they're female or male. Both prefer the rocky ledges of the park rather than the lush grasslands that elk and deer savor.

Sheep have a complex stomach and digestive system that lets them eat a wide variety of foods that they forage among the rocks. They often feed during the early hours, and then retreat to rock ledges to relax and re-chew their cud.

These nimble animals are well adapted to life in Rocky. They have a special hoof that lets them walk or jump easily among rocks, and they possess sharp eyesight, a keen sense of smell and acute hearing.

Rocky Mountain bighorn sheep don't have antlers like deer or elk do. They have true horns, sometimes weighing up to 15 pounds, which never fall off. The

Rocky Mountain Bighorn Sheep

males grow the curlicues most often photographed, while the ewe's horns look more like spikes.

The males and females stay in separate herds until mating time comes around from November to January.

Fall River Road

interpret wildflowers, fishing, hiking, wildlife, human habitation, birdwatching and weather patterns in Rocky Mountain National Park.

Old Fall River Road

"No trailers and no vehicles longer than 25 feet." That's how the park service sums up their requirement for vehicles on this tightly wound, switchback-prone, gravel, uphill one-way road. Don't let it scare you off, however. Indeed, the turns are tight but the road is wide and well-maintained. While ruts might work their way into the turns by summer's end, the levels and straights are rarely potholed or even washboarded. The rewards far outweigh any minor driving discomfort.

This old road shadows a glacially carved river valley

from Ponderosa parkland meadows, through an old-growth subalpine forest and crests the treeline into the heart of Rocky's alpine tundra. Mountains loom on both sides; to the left is the glistening Sundance Mountain, to the right are the snowy peaks of the Mummy Range that silhouette Colorado's usually delft-blue sky. Herds of elk are as close to guaranteed as nature ever gets. Bighorn sheep, American dippers, hawks and deer are everyday accompaniments to a cruise along this scenic gravel byway.

The road begins at the west end of Horseshoe Park, two miles west of the Fall River Entrance Station or 1.6 miles northwest of Deer Ridge Junction. For the first two miles—until Endovalley—Fall River is a regular two-way blacktop road. At Endovalley

it becomes a gravel, one-way thoroughfare for 9.5 miles, climbing to the Alpine Visitor Center.

History of Old Fall River Road

The Arapaho who used this byway called it the "Dog's Trail" since they had their dogs pull travois (sticks laid along the animals' sides and fitted with hide to carry loads) along the route. These natives traipsed the area frequently, migrating from the plains across the mountains to spend summers in the wildlife-filled parks.

Old Fall River Road was the first to top the Continental Divide in this part of the state. When construction began in 1913, promoters hoped to have the link to Grand Lake complete within two years, but it took seven. Fall River finally opened in 1920, five years after the park's founding, only to be closed in 1953 because of its high maintenance. It was re-opened in 1968.

Lawn Lake Trailhead

This trailhead leads to many of the larger lakes in the park, including Crystal and Ypsilon. Just east of the parking lot is the pleasant meadow where Rocky Mountain National Park was officially founded in a ceremony on September 4, 1915.

The many meadows along both sides of the road are frequent gathering locations for elk in the autumn months. The males "bugle" and joust each other for females.

Alluvial Fan

In the early morning hours of July 15, 1982, the earth dam at Lawn Lake burst about four miles north of this location. A surge of water nearly 30 feet high—and bristling with debris—roared downstream, scouring the valley walls. When the flood crashed through this moraine, it dropped thousands of tons of rock and debris in the shape of a fan as it spread out on the valley floor.

Today, a half-mile asphalt path crosses this alluvium, allowing visitors to gain a sense of what massive boulders can be moved by a wall of water. A beautiful waterfall resulted where the water broke through the moraine.

Unfortunately, even though there was adequate warning that the flood was raging down the valley, three campers at Aspenglen Campground were killed and $26 million damage was done to

downtown Estes Park.

Endovalley

This lovely picnic area has many tables sprinkled about among aspen and pine trees. Restrooms are available.

Endovalley is a tranquil, forested domain perfect for absorbing the beauty of a mixed riparian and subalpine ecosystem. Subalpine fir, Engelmann spruce, aspen and Ponderosa pine mix effortlessly. Fall River bubbles only a few steps away along paths forged through thick willow wetlands. At the river, American dippers feed on insect larvae below the water, hawks often float overhead and the serenity of life in Rocky settles in.

Old Fall River Road

At Endovalley, the one-way, uphill-only Fall River Road begins. No trailers are allowed, nor are vehicles longer than 25 feet. About a third of a mile up, a pullover on the left provides a wide-angle view of Horseshoe Park, including the lake formed by the 1982 flood.

Up-valley hangs the lower lip of Hanging Valley, which was cut when a higher glacier flows into a lower one.

The pullover at the first switchback lies next to a lovely spot where the water forms many small pools and short waterfalls as Fall River works its way down.

Notice the building-sized round granite domes at the second switchback. These are Silver Plume granite, formed 1.4 billion years ago.

Chasm Falls

The steep trail that leads down to these falls rewards visitors with a spray of water, squeezed tight between immense boulders. Dropping about 30 feet or so, the water and several rocks have burrowed a deep hole in the rock at the bottom of the falls

Sundance Mountain

As the forest disappears downslope of the road, Sundance Mountain reveals itself across the valley. Named by a miner who enjoyed watching

Dude Ranches

Some folks get a hankerin' to do some dude ranchin' after they've explored the park for a spell. Here's where to settle in: *Aspen Canyon Ranch;* (800-321-1357)—"Kid cowboy" program, riverside hottub, western cuisine and a drop-dead view. *Bar Lazy J Guest Ranch;* (970-725-3437 or 800-396-6279)—Horseback riding, horseshoe pitching, four-wheel-drive tours, mountain biking and gold medal fishing. *C Lazy U Ranch;* (970-887-

3344)—The only five-star, five-diamond-rated ranch in the world. *Drowsy Water;* (970-725-3456 or 800-845-2292)—Full riding instruction, children's programs, daily entertainment, overnights, cookouts, cabin or lodge accommodations and a heated pool. *Latigo Ranch;* (970-724-9008 or 800-227-9655)—200 miles of trails, horseback and cowboy skills taught in summer and cross-country skiing and snowshoeing when the snow flies.

Chasm Falls

There are frequently elk in the lower basin of the cirque. They sometimes lie among the wind-blown willows or gather together in open areas to enjoy the sunshine.

On the other side of the road, a path snakes out onto the alpine tundra. The park requests that walkers stay on the path, as any damage to the plants may actually take hundreds of years to repair.

From mid-June to mid-July, much of this tundra tickles the bright blue sky with a rainbow of wildflowers. Green chiming bells, yellow alpine avens, white American bisort, pink moss campion and old-man-on-the mountain enrapture visitors who brave the wind for a moment of meditation on the tundra.

Marmot Point

A small pullover on the right, located as the road crests the cirque toward the visitors center, is a favorite place to observe yellow-bellied marmots up close. Unfortunately, the reason they come so close is to get human food. Marmots have extremely sharp teeth and can be rather aggressive, so please don't feed them.

the sunlight dance across the acres of rock on its flanks, the top of Sundance is high in the alpine tundra.

Also visible is a large hourglass-shaped avalanche zone; notice the fallen trees on the right. Young aspen—often the first tree to grow after a disaster—are filling in on the left.

Willow Park

A small glacier that melted only about 6,500 years ago carved this willow-choked area. This is an excellent area for spotting elk and it provides a dramatic glimpse of the Fall River cirque, just below the Alpine Visitor Center.

Fall River Cirque

Parking is adequate on either end of the switchback that runs along this immense bowl.

The cirque has been the starting point for many glaciers, including the one that transformed Fall River Valley from a steep-sided, narrow chasm into the broad, curved route that the road ascends.

Grand Lake

Grand Lake

I f Estes Park is Rocky Mountain National Park's eager-to-greet-you front door, Grand Lake is the pull-out-the-toys-and-let's-play backyard. In Grand Lake, visitors may do many of the things forbidden in the park itself. You may guide your speed boat around a lake hauling a water skier,

pedal your bike on dirt trails in the wilderness, keep most of the fish you catch and paddle your kayak or drive your all-terrain vehicle almost anywhere you please.

Don't get the idea that Grand Lake is a break-the-rules frontier town. Quite the contrary, it's very law abiding. It's just that they savor the bounty around them.

History

While the Ute and Arapaho hunted and fished this rich region for generations, they fought over it too. On one occasion, according to

legend, when the Ute were outnumbered during a pitched battle, they put women and children in a raft and pushed them onto the lake and out of harm's way—or so they thought. As often happens in Colorado's high country, an afternoon squall came up, capsizing the makeshift craft and drowning all those aboard. From that time on, the Ute believed that the mists that drift off the lake on chilly summer mornings were the spirits of their lost loved ones. This explains Grand Lake's other moniker, Spirit Lake.

After a short-lived gold boom in the early 1880s, Grand Lake found its niche as a hunting and fishing paradise for wealthy Colorado families, who built cabins around the lake. By 1905, the highest elevation yacht club in the world was registered.

Grand Lake—the largest natural lake in Colorado—was dwarfed in 1952 by the construction of nearby Shadow Mountain Lake and Lake Granby. Together, the three lakes form the triple crown of Colorado's high-altitude water playgrounds.

left: Grand Lake's boardwalk

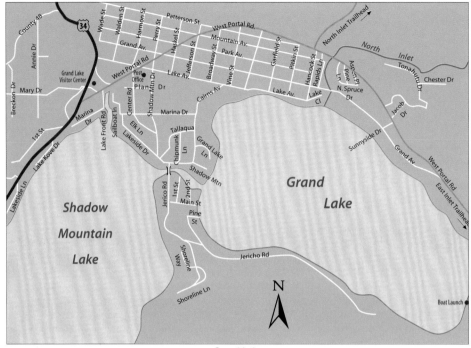

Grand Lake

Layout

Grand Lake nuzzles between the eastern shore of the lake and the western border of Rocky Mountain National Park. Many folks expect to find Grand Avenue (the main drag) straddling U.S. Highway 34, but you must actually turn east onto West Portal Road (a highway sign marks the turn) and then turn again to find Grand Lake. Newer homes and condominium developments nestle on the land bridge between Grand Lake and Shadow Mountain Reservoir. The older part of Grand Lake, which is the heart of town, runs east and west along Grand Avenue. The lake itself washes ashore one block south on Lake Avenue.

Grand Lake Visitor Center

A friendly group of people staff and stock the visitor center, located in the Chamber of Commerce building at the intersection of U.S. Highway 34 and West Portal Road; call 970-627-3402 or for a vacation planning packet, 800-531-1019.

Contemporary Aspects

Grand Lake is one city that's mighty comfortable with itself. And why not? They have a broad main street called Grand Avenue, which is banded with boardwalks, and fragrant fir and pine accent many corners. Just a block off Grand Avenue, Colorado's largest natural lake sports

Grand Lake Lodge

A few things in life fall into the "must-see" category. One of these is the view from the Grand Lake Lodge (970-627-3967 or 303-759-5848). Built in 1920 as one of a trio of hotels, the lodge occupies the one spot that has a view of the village of Grand Lake itself and the three lakes near it.

Weary visitors often find themselves lounging back into one of their rocking chairs, hitching their legs up onto the lodgepole pine railing and lolling the afternoon away.

Open only during summer, the clean and simple lodge's cabins fall into the rustic category. Dinner in the exposed log dining room is a different story. Expect well-prepared fish, game and beef.

boats and fishers who enjoy themselves mightily.

True western facades line the streets: parapets step up and down, gables slide hither and yon. A handsome log community center looks over a grassy park, where children play soccer and a gazebo attracts folks who need to sit down for a minute and relax on their vacation.

Grand Lake is a city built to host visitors. Restaurant options run the gamut from "Why?" to "Wow!," dozens of motels provide clean, simple rooms, condominiums and historic hotels fill the "rustic-but-rich" niche and a day of shopping calls from behind split-log storefronts. They even have two putt-putt golf courses and a human maze.

Attractions

Grand Lake is rich with things to do, most of them recreational. However, for a day away from the water (or Rocky Mountain National Park), the first order of business is a stroll along the boardwalks lining Grand Avenue. The walkway itself is a bit of an attraction: it's one of the few boardwalks in the state. Every few yards, a gas lamp reminds visitors of days gone by, but more interestingly, each of the lamps sprouts from a small garden planted and maintained by a local green thumb. These alpine wonders boast just

Grand Lake Festival and Annual Events

January
Winter Carnival: Chilly but fun activities. Various locations; call 970-627-3402.
Ice Fishing Derby: Ice fishing for prizes. Grand Lake; call 970-887-9344.
January/February
Winterfest: Snowmobile activities throughout the winter months include drag races, mini-snowmobile races on the lake, concerts, snow sculpture. Various locations; call 970-627-3402.
February
Goosebump Open Ice Golf Tournament: Ice putting and tennis ball frivolity. Grand Lake; admission; call 970-627-3402.
March
High Altitude Sled Dog Championships: Mush those huskies. Winding River Resort; parking fee; call 970-627-3402.
May
Spring Fishing Derby: Catch a big one, win a prize. Various locations; fee; call 970-887-9344.
Memorial Day Weekend Celebration: Parade, observance,

silent auction. Town Park; free; call 970-627-3402.
June/August
Rocky Mountain Repertory Theater: Community Building. Nightly; admission; call 970-627-3402.
July
Fourth of July Fireworks: Still perhaps the largest on Western Slope. Grand Lake; donations accepted; call 970-627-3402.
Wooden Boat Show: Grand Lake Yacht Club. Admission; call 970-627-3377.
Annual Chili Cook-off-on-the-Beach: Grand Lake. Admission; call 970-627-3402.
Western Week: A mountain man rendezvous, shootouts, buffalo BBQ and parade. Call 970-627-3402.
August
Annual Rubber Duckie Races: Family festival and charity event. Columbine Creek Ranch; call 970-627-3402.
Grand Lake Regatta & Lipton Cub Races: High-altitude yacht racing. Grand Lake Yacht Club; call 970-627-3377.

Daven Haven Downs Turtle Races: Dress up a turtle and watch it run. Daven Haven Lodge; admission; call 970-627-8144.
Food and Wine Festival: Grand Lake Yacht Club. Admission; call 970-627-3402.
Fine Arts and Fine Crafts Festival: Adjacent to Grand Lake Yacht Club; free; call 970-627-3402.
September
Arts and Crafts Fair: Celebrates the changing of the aspen trees. Town Park; call 970-627-3402.
September/October
Concert in the Pines: Held in historic Community House. Donation; call 970-627-3402.
October Trail of Terror and Haunted House: Columbine Creek Ranch. Admission; call 970-627-3402.
December
Old Fashioned Christmas: Santa, melodrama, sleigh rides, caroling, live Nativity play, figure skating, snowman contest. Admission for melodrama only; call 970-627-3402.

Shadow Mountain Reservoir

about every annual that can survive at this altitude. Some gardeners keep their plots simple, merely planting a few geraniums. Others plant elaborate marvels that feature something in bloom all summer long.

The stores themselves sell a wide range of goods. Anticipate troves of trinkets and T-shirts, reasonably priced camping and outfitting goods and a range of affordable arts and crafts.

The only museum on the lake is, literally, right on the lakeshore. The Kaufmann House Museum is really a restored hotel that provides a glimpse of what life was like for the people who lived here around the turn of the century.

Recreation

Outdoor fun, summer and winter, is the reason people come to the Grand Lake area. Grand Lake, Shadow Mountain Lake and Lake Granby offer nearly every sport that can take place on the water. And the three lakes are surrounded by wilderness:

Camping in Grand Lake		
Campground	**Tent/RV Sites**	**Season**
Elk Creek Campground 970-627-8502 or 800-355-2733	33 RV 36 tents	Year-round
Winding River Resort 970-627-3215 or 303-623-1121	115 RV 40 tents	Year-round
Arapaho Bay Campground 800-280-2267	84	Summer
Green Ridge Campground 800-280-2267	78	Summer
Stillwater Campground 800-280-2267	127	Summer
Willow Creek Campground 800-280-2267	35	Summer

Grand Lake Marina

to the east, south and north are Rocky Mountain National Park; to the west lies the Arapaho National Forest; to the southeast is the Indian Peaks Wilderness. It shouldn't come as a surprise that folks here are very active.

Hiking

The hundreds of miles of wilderness surrounding Grand Lake offer dozens of opportunities for hikes of any length and complexity. Some

of the easiest and enjoyable are nearby in Rocky Mountain National Park. Near Grand Lake are two trailheads that lead hikers into the wilderness.

Tonahutu/North Inlet Trailhead

Tonahutu is the starting point for several moderate and difficult hikes deep into the least-used portions of Rocky. Several horse outfitters use these trails to take guests into

the backcountry.

A relatively level (but long) hike takes walkers to a popular meadow: Summerland Park.

East Inlet Trailhead

This is the trailhead used by the renowned, one-armed explorer Major John Wesley Powell and *Rocky Mountain News* publisher William Byers when they made the first successful ascent of Longs Peak in August, 1868. Byers' stories about his adventures convinced many east coast readers to come out west to experience the delights of Colorado themselves.

The course they took is a long and arduous one, but an exploration along the first few miles reveals some delights. About a third of a mile along this rolling trail, Adams Falls crashes down a narrow cleft of rock. Beyond, the trail echoes the river's course through lodgepole pine and aspen to some wildflower

Children's Activities in Grand Lake

- Pony rides are available at the Sombrero Stables (970-627-3514).
- Winding River Resort (970-627-3215) offers several kid-friendly activities. Pony rides are popular, but so is the hay ride—a "musical" wagon takes folks to the Sasparilla Saloon. Barn animals are on site for petting, too.
- Rocky Mountain National Park

has an almost unlimited number of educational programs for kids. For a listing, consult the *High Country Headlines*, available at visitor centers and ranger stations in the park.
- Kids love the Alpine Slide at Winter Park (970-726-5514). It sails around 26 turns as it scoots along 3,030 feet of track and drops 630 vertical feet.

spangled meadows. To get started, follow West Portal Road and look for the marked parking lot on the left where the road turns to gravel.

Colorado River Trailhead

A long but level walk leads to Lulu City (a ghost town) from this trailhead, which lies inside Rocky itself. The Never Summer Ranch, located alongside the Colorado River, is a half-mile

walk back into history—the ranch was a turn-of-the-century dude ranch. Both these hikes require admission into the park.

Most of the hiking in the national forest and the wilderness area is moderate to difficult. For information, ask at the visitor center or at one of the mountain equipment stores in downtown Grand Lake.

Bicycling

There are hundreds of miles of mountain bike trails in Grand County, and more than 100 miles in the Grand Lake vicinity alone. The visitor center distributes a brochure, *Grand Lake Mountain Bike Trail Map*, with most of the trails outlined. For a bicycle rental, try Rocky Mountain Sports on Grand Avenue in Grand Lake; call 970-627-8124.

The nearby ski resort of Winter Park (970-726-5514) is worth checking out if you're a bike enthusiast. The resort boasts 600 miles of fat-tire trails.

Snowmobiling

Quite simply, Grand Lake is Colorado's snowmobiling capital. With more than 150 miles of groomed trails, Grand Lake claims to have more groomed runs than any spot in the region. A "run" may be a simple trail or an elaborate hill-climbing area. Snowmobilers may

even ride into Rocky Mountain National Park itself as far as the Milner Pass/Continental Divide pull-off, although the fact that the noise wrecks havoc on the animals' nerves is becoming controversial. Several shops rent equipment, suits and helmets; try Spirit Lake Rentals (970-627-9288) or On The Trail Snowmobile Rental (970-627-2429).

Cross-country Skiing

Gaining popularity in the state, stride skiing is well established here. The Ski Touring Center, located at Grand Lake Golf Course (970-627-8008), equips skiers with skis, poles, lessons and maps. They also have miles of groomed trails skirting in and out of trees and along rivers. Many skiers enjoy cross-country skiing in Rocky itself. The most popular trail is the lovely (and nearly level) trail to Lulu City from the Colorado River Trailhead.

Downhill Skiing

Downhill skiers often stay in Grand Lake to ski at Silver Creek or Winter Park because the room rates are lower. Also, the drive, about 20 or 35 miles, is well maintained in winter.

Bald Eagle

Golf

At an elevation of 8,420 feet above sea level, the Grand Lake Golf Course (970-627-8008) is one of the highest in the country. This 18-hole course has narrow and luxuriously forested fairways and greens that can be frustrating until the secret of how they break is decoded.

Tennis

Tennis is free in Grand Lake at courts located at the golf course and in town.

Boat Rental

A trip to the lakes is hardly a getaway without getting out on the water. The Spirit Lake Marina (970-627-8158) rents a variety of boats by the hour or day to sail, motor or paddle your way out on Grand Lake.

Jeep Tours

Four-wheel drive vehicles jostle their way across the Continental Divide during the summer. To sign up, call Mad Adventures at 970-726-5290 or 800-451-4844.

Moose

Fishing

A stretch of Colorado's Gold Medal water—a program devoted to highlighting Colorado's finest fishing—runs from Windy Gap to Troublesome Creek. This 20-mile stretch along U.S. Highway 40, between Hot Sulphur Springs and Kremmling, provides terrific casting opportunities for rainbow and brown trout.

The lakes themselves also offer rainbow and brown as well as mackinaws and Kokanee salmon. Rent a boat or tube at Spirit Lake Marina (970-627-8158). A license is required by all fishers 16 years old or older.

Nightlife

Many folks find themselves after a day or two in the west with a hankering to step lively to a country western two-step. In these parts, those folks head to the Stagecoach Inn (970-627-9932) or Grumpy's (970-627-3149) for live music and a dance floor. Locals have been discovered tying up their horses at the Lariat (970-627-9965) before they step in for a drink.

For more of a sit-down amusement, the Rocky Mountain Repertory Theater produces live and well-reviewed stage shows nightly through the summer at the Community Hall; call 970-627-3421.

Horseback Riding

On land that shares a border with Rocky Mountain National Park, Sombrero Ranch (970-627-3514) saddles up riders for many different kinds and lengths of outings. They offer pony trots for children as well as one-hour, two-hour, half-day, full-day and multi-day excursions. Breakfast and sunset-dinner rides are also popular. Winding River Resort (970-627-3215) offers one- and two-hour trail rides in addition to hay rides.

River Rafting

The river rafting in these parts is downstream along the mighty Colorado River. Try Mad Adventures (970-726-5290 or 800-451-4844) or Monarch Guides (888-GO-FLOAT) for trips that raft the roiling river beyond Kremmling.

following page: Sprague Lake

Reference

Accommodations

Accommodation listings are arranged alphabetically by city. Following the city roster are lodging associations which can also recommend accommodations. Price classifications are based upon single-night summer rates, double occupancy and do not include taxes: $ = under $50; $$ = $50 to $99; $$$ = $100 to $150; $$$$ = $150 and above. Reservations are always suggested for summer stays, which often book up months in advance. Not all the properties listed are open year-round.

Estes Park Hotels

All Budget Inn, 945 Moraine Route, U.S. Hwy. 36 West, Estes Park, CO 80517; call 970-586-3485 or 800-628-3438. Rates $$, 15 units. Mini-kitchens, microwaves, cable TV.

Alpenaire Inn, 215 Virginia Drive, Box 1594, Estes Park, CO 80517; call 970-586-6607 or 800-668-0301, FAX 970-586-6607. Rates $$ to $$$, 6 units. Casual country inn charm in c.1909 house or cabins.

Alpine Trail Ridge Inn, 927 Moraine Route, Estes Park, CO 80517; call 970-586-4585 or 800-233-5023, FAX 970-586-6249. Rates $$, 48 units. Some private balconies, pool and restaurant.

Amberwood, 1889 Fall River Road, Estes Park, CO 80517; call 970/ 586-4385. Rates $$ to $$$$, 17 units. Cottages and lodge rooms, kitchens, microwaves, cable TV, some fireplaces.

American Wilderness Lodge, 481 W. Elkhorn, Estes Park, CO 80517; call 970-586-4402 or 800-ROCKY MT, Ext. 220. Rates $$, 33 units. Riverside location, balconies, fireplaces, kitchens, TV, heated pool, sauna, hot tubs, pets welcome.

Anniversary Inn, 1060 Mary's Lake Road, Moraine Route, Estes Park, CO 80517; call 970-586-6200. Rates $$ to $$$, 4 units. Bed and breakfast in turn-of-the-century log home.

Aspen Lodge Ranch Resort, 6120 Hwy. 7, LPR, Estes Park, CO 80517; call or FAX 970-586-8133. Package rates only. Log lodge and cabins bordering Rocky Mountain National Park.

Baldpate Inn, 4900 South Hwy. 7, P.O. Box 4445, Estes Park, CO 80517; Rates $$; call 970-586-6151. Rustic lodge and cabins, restaurant.

Best Western at Lake Estes Resort, 1650 Big Thompson Hwy. Box 1466C, Estes Park, CO 80517; call 970-586-3386 or 800-292-VIEW, FAX 970-586-9000. Rates $$ to $$$$, 58 units. AAA three diamond, great views, kitchens, fireplaces, Jacuzzi.

Big Thompson Timberlane Lodge, Box 387, Hwy. 36 West, Estes Park, CO 80517; call 970-586-3137. Rates $$ to $$$$, 37 units. Secluded individual log homes, cottages and motel units on five acres, swimming pool, hot tubs and whirlpool, fireplaces, cable TV.

Black Canyon Inn, 800 MacGregor Ave., P.O. Box 856, Estes Park, CO 80517; call 970-586-3154. Rates $$ to $$$, 25 units. Suites, fireplaces, kitchens, indoor spa and outdoor pool.

Black Dog Inn Bed & Breakfast, P.O. Box 4659, 650 South St. Vrain Ave., Estes Park, CO 80517; call 970-586-0374. Rates $$ to $$$, 4 units. Restored 1904 mountain home, antique furnishings, whirlpool tub, fireplaces.

Blackhawk Lodges, 1750 Fall River Road, Estes Park, CO 80517; call 970-586-6100. Rates $$ to $$$, 10 units. Log cabins, kitchens, fireplaces, cable TV and hot tub.

Boulder Brook, 1900 Fall River Road, Estes Park, CO 80517; call 970-586-0910. Rates $$ to $$$, 16 units. Contemporary suites, in-room spas, fireplaces, cable TV, cooking facilities.

Brynwood on the River, 710 Moraine Ave., P.O. Box 1929, Estes Park, CO 80517; call 970-586-3475 or 800-279-4488. Rates $$ to $$$$, 28 units. Family resort, river cottages or motel, hot tubs and pool.

Castle Mountain Lodge, 1520 Fall River Road, Estes Park, CO 80517; call 970-586-3664, FAX 970-586-6060. Rates $$ to $$$$, 30 units. Riverside cottages and vacation homes with kitchens, fireplaces, cable TV.

Colorado Cottages, 1241 High Drive, Moraine Route, Estes Park, CO 80517; call 970-586-4637 or 800-486-1236. Rates $$ to $$$, 11 units. Housekeeping cottages, kitchens, fireplaces, cable TV.

Columbine Inn, 1540 Big Thompson, P.O. Box 1635, Estes Park, CO 80517; call 970-586-4533 or 800-726-9049. Rates $$, 18 units. Fireplaces, microwaves, refrigerators, cable TV.

Comfort Inn, 1450 Big Thompson Ave., Box 393, Estes Park, CO 80517; call 970-586-2358 or 800-228-5150. Rates $$ to $$$, 75 units. Some balconies, pool, whirlpool and A/C.

Deer Crest, P.O. Box 1768, Estes Park, CO 80517; call 970-586-2324 or 800-331-2324, FAX 970-586-8693. Rates $$, 26 units. AAA three diamond, riverfront setting, refrigerators, microwaves, cable TV, balconies/patios, heated pool.

Eagle Cliff Bed & Breakfast, 2383 Hwy. 66, Box 4312, Estes Park, CO 80517; call 970-586-5425. Rates $$ to $$$, 3 units. Small bed and breakfast within walking distance of Rocky Mountain National Park.

Holiday Inn of Estes Park, 101 South St. Vrain, Box 1468, Estes Park, CO 80517; call 970-586-2332 or 800-80-ESTES, FAX 970-586-2332. Rates $$ to $$$, 150 units. Holidome, indoor pool, whirlpool, fitness room, restaurant.

Inn at Estes Park, 1701 Big Thompson Ave., P.O. Box 1408, Estes Park, CO 80517; call 970-586-5363 or 800-458-1182, FAX 970-586-5363. Rates $$ to $$$, 145 units. Indoor pool, hot tub, sauna, some balconies, A/C.

Lane Guest Ranch, P.O. Box 1766, Estes Park, CO 80517;

call 970-747-2493. Rates $$$, 25 units. All-inclusive, horseback riding , jeep trips, swimming pool, fishing guide, evening entertainment.

Lazy R Cottages, P.O. Box 1996, Estes Park, CO 80517; call 970-586-3708 or 800-726-3728. Rates $$ to $$$$, 14 units. Knotty pine cabins, great views, fireplaces, hot tubs, cable TV, kitchens, grills and picnic tables.

Machin's Cottages in the Pines, P.O. Box 2687CW, Estes Park, CO 80517; call 970-586-4276. Rates $$ to $$$, 17 units. Secluded cottages within Rocky Mountain National Park, fireplaces, kitchens, cable TV.

McGregor Mountain Lodge, 2815 Fall River Road, Estes Park, CO 80517; call 970-586-3457, FAX 970-586-4040. Rates $$$ to $$$$, 19 units. Cottages, suites with kitchens and fireplaces.

Miles Motel and Cottages, 1250 South St. Vrain, Estes Park, CO 80517; call 970-586-3185. Rates $$, 19 units. Housekeeping units and a four-bedroom cottage, some with fireplaces, cable TV.

Ponderosa Lodge, 1820 Fall River Road MR, Estes Park, CO 80517; call 970-586-4233 or 800-628-0512. Rates $$ to $$$$, 19 units. AAA three diamond, riverfront balconies, fireplaces, kitchenettes, HBO.

Rams Horn Village Resort, 1565 Hwy. 66, Estes Park, CO 80517; call 970-586-4338 or 800-229-4676, FAX 970-586-4689. Rates $$ to $$$$. Great views, luxury vacation homes and rustic cottages, pool, hot tubs, some

fireplaces.

Romantic Riversong Bed & Breakfast Inn, P.O. Box 1910, Estes Park, CO 80517; call 970-586-4666. Rates $$$ to $$$$, 9 units. Country inn on 27 acres, whirlpool tubs and fireplaces.

Saddle and Surrey Motel, 1341 South St. Vrain, Estes Park, CO 80517; call 970-586-3326, FAX 970-586-3326. Rates $ to $$, 26 units. Some kitchens, pool, spa, cable TV.

Silver Saddle Lodge, 1260 Big Thompson Ave., P.O. Box 1747, Estes Park, CO 80517; call or FAX 970-586-4476. Rates $$ to $$$, 54 units. AAA three diamond, pool, whirlpool, some balconies, kitchens.

The Stanley Hotel & Conference Center, 333 Wonderview Ave., P.O. Box 1767, Estes Park, CO 80517; call 970-586-3371 or 800-976-1377. Rates $$$$, 133 units. Elegant Georgian-style hotel with full conference facilities, pool, two fine-dining restaurants.

Streamside . . . A Village of Cabin Suites, 1260 Fall River Road, Box 2930, Estes Park, CO 80517; call 970-586-6464 or 800-321-3303, FAX 970-586-6272. Rates $$$$, 19 units. AAA four diamond property on 17 acres.

Sunnyside Knoll Resort, 1675 Fall River Road, Estes Park, CO 80517; call 970-586-5759 or 800-586-5212. Rates $$ to $$$$, 15 units. Suites with Jacuzzis, fireplaces, cable TV, outdoor hot tub and heated pool. No children under 12.

Timberline Motel & Cottages, 455 South St. Vrain, P.O. Box 106, Estes Park, CO 80517; call 970-586-4697 or 800-

274-4697. Rates $$, 25 units. Motel rooms and cottages, pool, some kitchens and fireplaces, cable TV.

Tiny Town Cottages, 830 Moraine Route, Estes Park, CO 80517; call 970-586-4249. Rates $ to $$, 20 units. Two-person cottages, kitchen, fireplaces, cable TV.

Trails West on the River, 1710 Fall River Road, Estes Park, CO 80517; call 970-586-4629. Rates $$ to $$$, 19 units. Suites or cabins, fireplaces, hot tub, cable TV.

Triple R Cottages, 1000 Riverside Drive, Estes Park, CO 80517. Rates $ to $$$, 7 units. Housekeeping cottages, cable TV, kitchenettes, grills, picnic area and playground.

Valhalla Resort, P.O. Box 1439, Estes Park, CO 80517; call 970-586-3284, FAX 970-586-6361. Rates $$ to $$$$, 22 units. Vacation homes and rustic cottages, fireplaces, cable TV, pool and hot tub.

Wildwood Inn, 2801 Fall River Road, Estes Park, CO 80517; call 970-586-2933. Rates $ to $$$$, 16 units. Condo suites, in-room spas, fireplaces and private decks.

Woodlands on Fall River, 1888 Fall River Road, Estes Park, CO 80517; call 970-586-0404 , FAX 970-586-3297. Rates $$$, 16 units. Condominium suites, private deck and patios, kitchens, fireplaces, cable TV.

Grand Lake Hotels

Beacon Landing Motel and Marina, 1026 County Rd. 64, Granby, CO, 80446; call 970-627-3671 or 800-864-4372. Rates $$ to $$$, 10 rooms, one and two bedroom units, rustic kitchenettes, no pets, mountain views.

Bighorn Lodge, 613 Grand Ave., Grand Lake, CO 80447; call 970-627-8101 or 800-341-8000. Rates $$ to $$$$, 20 rooms, Queen-sized beds, hot tub, walk to anywhere in town.

Brownhurst Cabins, P. O. Box 97, Grand Lake, CO 80447; call 970-627-3410. Rates $ to $$, 10 rustic cabins on the east end of Grand Lake, showers, carpeted, color cable TV, fireplaces in five units.

Daven Haven Lodge and Cabins, P. O. Box 1528, Grand Lake, CO 80447; call 970-627-8144 or 970-627-8746. Rates $$ to $$$, 12 cabins, no kitchens, cable TV, heated outdoor pool, in town, banquet facilities, restaurant and lounge.

Driftwood Lodge, 12255 U.S. Hwy. 34, Box 609, Grand Lake, CO 80447; phone and FAX 970-627-3654. Rates $$, 19 units. Swimming pool, sauna, whirlpool and playground.

Eagle's Landing and Eagle's Spirit Condominiums, 902 Grand Avenue, Grand Lake CO; call 970-627-3425 or 800/252-3425. Rates $$$ to $$$$, two and three bedroom units, spa in each unit, fireplaces, private decks with lake view.

Fanning's Cabin, contact C. J. Fanning, 9742 W. 67 Place, Arvada, CO 80004; call 303-424-1625. Rates $$$, two-night minimum, fully furnished three bedroom, one full bath cabin in the village of Grand Lake, walking distance to downtown.

Gala Marina and Motel, 928 County Road 64, Granby, CO 80446; call 970-627-3220.

Rates $$, one and two bedroom units, lake-front cabin-like structures with kitchenettes, cable TV, panoramic views.

Grand Lake Lodge, 15500 US Hwy. 34, Box 569, Grand Lake, CO 80447; call 303-759-5848 or 970-627-3937, FAX 303-759-3179 or 970-627-9495. Rates $$ to $$$$, 56 units. National historic landmark, rustic cabins, pool, entertainment, restaurant.

Grandview Lodge, 12429 Hwy. 34, Grand Lake, CO 80447; call 970-627-3914. Rates $, just outside downtown Grand Lake, micro-fridges, grilles, cable TV, playground, deck, pets welcome, open all year.

Inn at Grand Lake, Inc., 1103 Grand Ave., Grand Lake, CO 80447; call 970-627-9234 or 800-722-2585. Rates $ to $$, economical lodging in an Old West setting, one block from lake, rustic mountain lodge with all the comforts.

Lemmon Lodge, P.O. Box 514, Grand Lake, CO 80447; call 970-627-3314 or 970-725-3511. Rates $$ to $$$$, lake-front property with private beach, in town, kitchens, color cable TV, private boat docks, some fireplaces.

Lonesome Dove Cottages, 416 Grand Ave., Grand Lake, CO 80447; call 970-627-8019. Rates $$ to $$$, 8 cottages with fully equipped kitchens, TV, VCR, close to town, outdoor hot tub, snowmobile rental, two bedroom available.

Lone Eagle Lodge, 712 Grand Ave., Grand Lake, CO 80447; call 970-627-3310 or 800-282-3311. Rate $$, 12 one or two bedroom units two

blocks from the lake, hot tub, spacious deck, picnic area, log cabin atmosphere.
Mountain Lakes Lodge, 10480 U.S. Hwy. 34, Grand Lake, CO 80447; call 970-627-8448. Rates $ to $$$, 10 cozy, rustic cabins and two houses, log-vaulted ceilings, kitchenettes, most with woodstoves, cable TV, log homes for large groups.
Nonehshe Cabins, 450 Broadway, Grand Lake, CO 80447; call 970-627-8012. Rates $$, one bedroom cabins, furnished to sleep four, fully equipped kitchenettes, private picnic areas, BBQ grills, cable TV, open all year.
Pine Cone Cottages, 1025 Park Ave., Grand Lake, CO 80447; call 970-627-9454. Rates $$, 4 quaint, elegantly decorated cottages with seclusion in the middle of town, kitchenettes, next to park and conference facility, non-smoking, no pets, cable TV, VCR available.
Preisser's Lodge, contact 939 S. Milwaukee Way, Denver, CO; call 303-722-2528 or 970-627-8383. Rates $$ to $$$$, 5 buildings sleep between two and eight; on south shore of Grand Lake, open June to September, electric kitchens, heaters and fireplaces, sleeps two to eight, overlooks lake, private dock, no pets.
River Pines Cottages & RV Park, 12082 U.S. Hwy 34. Grand Lake, CO 80447; call 970-627-3632 or 800-793-0835. Rates $$ to $$$, 14 units, historic log cabins and condominiums on Colorado River, within walking distance of Shadow Mountain Lake, fully equipped kitchens, fireplaces, hot tub,

horseshoes, volleyball.
Rocky Mountain Cabins, P.O. Box 835, Grand Lake, CO 80447; call 970-627-3061. Rates $$ to $$$, 3 custom-designed log cabins located two miles south of Grand Lake, completely furnished kitchens, fireplaces, washer/dryer.
Spirit Lake Lodge, P.O. Box 66, Grand Lake, CO 80447; call 970-627-3344 or 800-544-6593. Rate $$, in town, easy access to activities, one and two bedroom units with full baths, heated pool, hot tub, parking.
Summit at Silver Creek Condominiums, 207 Lake Drive, Silver Creek, CO; call 888-482-7544. Rates $$ to $$$$, fully furnished condominiums fifteen minutes from Grand Lake, studio to two-bedroom with lofts, cable TV, fireplaces, hot tubs, full kitchen, private decks.
Trails End, P. O. Box 14, Grand Lake, CO 80447; call 970-627-8027 or 303-296-1949. Rates $$$$ with two-night minimum, attractively furnished and decorated cabin overlooking Winding River Ranch, secluded, mountain view, two bedroom, one-and-one-half bath, fully equipped kitchen.
Waconda Motel and Restaurant, 725 Grand Ave., Grand Lake, CO 80447; call 970-627-8312. Rate $$, 10 rooms, family and two-room units, queen beds, cable TV, hot tub, high country hospitality, some rooms feature fireplaces.
Western Riviera Motel & Cabins, 419 Garfield Ave., Grand Lake, CO 80447; call 970-627-3580. Rates $$ to $$$, lake-

front property with swimming, boating and fishing within sight of your room, snowmobile parking, downtown location, close to restaurants.
Wildwood Cabins, 1201 Grand Ave., Grand Lake, CO 80447; call 970-627-8746 or 970-627-8144. Rates $$, 4 charming, cozy cabins located one block from the lake and a public beach, kitchens, fireplaces, cable TV.

Longmont Hotels
Briarwood Inn Motel, 1228 North Main, Longmont, CO 80501; call 303-776-6622, FAX 303-772-7453. Rates $$, 17 units. Centrally located, cable TV, kitchenettes, whirlpool spa, patio area and BBQ.
Raintree Plaza Hotel & Conference Center, 1900 Ken Pratt Blvd., Longmont, CO 80501; call 303-776-2000 or 800-843-8240, FAX 303-776-2000. Rates $$, 211 units. Concierge wing and mini-suites with refrigerator, wet bar and coffee maker, pool, gym, restaurant.

Loveland Hotels
Best Western Coach House Resort, 5542 East Hwy. 34, Loveland, CO 80537; call 970-667-7810. Rates $ to $$, 88 units. Mobil two stars, AAA three diamond, indoor/outdoor pool, whirlpool, tennis, picnic area, restaurant and lounge.

Associations
American Youth Hostels, Rocky Mountain Council, P.O. Box 2370, Boulder, CO 80306; call 303-442-1166. Association of Historic Hotels of the Rocky Mountain West, 1002 Walnut #201, Boulder,

CO 80302; call 303-546-9040.
Bed & Breakfast Innkeepers of
Colorado Association, P.O.
Box 38416, Dept. T96, Col-
orado Springs, CO 80937; call
800-83-BOOKS.
Colorado Association of
Campgrounds, Cabins &
Lodges, 5101 Pennsylvania
Avenue, Boulder, CO 80303;
call 303-499-9343.
Colorado Dude / Guest Ranch
Association, P.O. Box 300,
Tabernash, CO 80478; call
970-887-3128 or 970-724-
3653.
Colorado Hotel and Lodging
Association, 999 18th Street,
Suite1240, Denver, CO
80202; call 303-297-8335.
Distinctive Inns of Colorado,
P.O. Box 2061, Estes Park, CO
80517; call 800-866-0621.

Airports

Denver International Airport,
8500 Pena Blvd., Denver, CO
80249-6340; call 303-342-2250.
Regional airports are located
in Fort Collins and Loveland.
    For airport shuttle service,
call Emerald Taxi & Shuttle at
970-586-1992 or Charles Tour
& Travel at 970-586-5151.

Emergencies

Dial 911 to reach local emergency services. The Estes Park
Medical Center is a fully
staffed hospital with 24-hour
emergency service; call 970-
586-2317. The Grand Lake
Medical Center can be
reached at 970-627-8477.

Government Agencies

State Agencies

Colorado Division of Wildlife,
6060 Broadway, Denver, CO;
call 303-297-1192.

Colorado Geological Survey,
1313 Sherman St., #715,
Denver, CO 80203; call 303-
866-2611.
Colorado Historical Society,
1300 Broadway, Denver, CO
80023; call 303-866-3682.
Colorado State Parks, 1313
Sherman St., #618, Denver,
CO 80203; call 303-866-3437.
Colorado State Patrol, 700
Kipling, Denver, CO 80215;
call 303-239-4500.

Federal Agencies

Bureau of Land Management,
Colorado State Office, 2850
Youngfield St., Lakewood,
CO 80215; call 303-239-3600.
U.S. Fish & Wildlife Service,
P.O. Box 25486, DFC, Den-
ver, CO 80225; call 303-236-
7904.
U.S. Forest Service, P.O. Box
25127, Lakewood, CO 80225;
call 303-275-5350.
U.S. Geological Survey, Box
25046 Federal Center, Mail
Stop 504, Denver, CO 80225-
0046; call 303-202-4200.

National Forests

Arapaho / Roosevelt National
Forests, Pawnee National
Grassland, 1311 S. College
Ave., Fort Collins, CO 80524;
call 970-498-2770.
Boulder Ranger Station, Ara-
paho / Roosevelt National
Forests, 2995 Baseline, Rm.
110, Boulder, CO 80303; call
303-444-6600.
U.S. Forest Service Regional
Headquarters, 740 Simms
St., Lakewood, CO 80025; call
303-275-5350.

Restaurants

Restaurant prices are based on
a typical entrée, no drinks or
taxes: $ = under $20; $$ = $20
to $30; $$$ = over $30.

Estes Park Restaurants

Andrea's, 145 Elkhorn; call
970-586-0886. Prices $$. In-
ternational cuisine.
Baldpate Inn, 4900 Co. Hwy 7;
call 970-586-5397. Prices $.
Soup and salad buffet,
homemade bread.
Black Canyon Inn, 800 Mac-
Gregor Ave.; call 970-586-
9344. Prices $$ to $$$. Conti-
nental cuisine with a spe-
cialty in seafood.
Bunny's Buns, 184 E. Elkhorn
(on Riverwalk); call 970-586-
6918. Prices $. Cinnamon
buns, bagels, croissants and
ice cream.
Cowpoke Cafe, 165 Virginia
(Courtyard Shops); call 970-
586-0234. Prices $ to $$.
Hearty Western food with
salad bar.
Dunraven Inn, 2470 Co. Hwy.
66; call 970-586-6409. Prices
$$. Italian specialities and
fresh fish.
Ed's Cantina, 362 E. Elkhirn;
call 970-586-2919. Prices $.
Mexican food, broasted
chicken and salad bar.
Elkhorn Lodge Restaurant, 600
W. Elkhorn; call 970-586-
4416. Prices $$. Cowboy
breakfasts, steak and trout
dinners.
Estes Park Brewery, 470
Prospect Village Dr.; call 970-
586-5421. Prices $ to $$.
Burgers, brats and beer.
Friar's Restaurant, 157 Elkhorn
(Church Shops); call 970-
586-2806. Prices $ to $$.
American specialities includ-
ing hazelnut chicken.
Grumpy Gringo, 1560 Big
Thompson Ave., call 970-
586-7705. Prices $. Mexican
specialties.
Inn of Glen Haven, Devils
Gulch Rd.; call 970-586-3897.
Prices $$$. Fine dining, steak

and salmon specialties. La Chaumière, Hwy. 36 between Estes Park and Lyons; call 303-823-6521. Prices $$ to $$$. Smokehouse specialties, homemade ice cream.

Mama Rose's, 338 E. Elkhorn; call 970-586-3330. Prices $. Family-style Italian cooking.

Notchtop Cafe & Pub, Upper Stanley Village; call 970-586-0272. Prices $. Baked goods and sandwiches.

Other Side Restaurant, National Park Village; call 970-586-2171. Prices $ to $$. Steaks and seafood.

Poppy's Pizza & Grill, 342 E. Elkhorn (Barlow Plaza); call 970-586-8282. Prices $. Pizza, sandwiches, soup and salad bar.

The Stanley Hotel, 333 W. Wonderview Ave.; call 970-586-3371. Prices $$ to $$$. Two restaurants, the Dunraven Grille and the MacGregor Room; fine dining with American Continental cuisine.

Wild Basin Smorgasbord, 13 miles south of Estes Park on Hwy 7; call 303-747-2545. Prices $. Chicken and roast beef, soup and salad bar.

Grand Lake Restaurants

Caroline's Cuisine, 9921 U.S. Hwy 34; call 970-627-9404. Prices $ to $$. French and American cuisine, full bar, extensive wine list.

E.G.'s Garden Grill, 1000 Grand Ave.; call 970-627-8404. Prices $ to $$. Lunch and dinner, full range in menu from burgers to gourmet meals, ribs a specialty.

Grand Lake Lodge, 15500 U.S. Hwy 34; call 970-627-3185. Prices $ to $$$. Continental

cuisine with open grill, full breakfast buffet, meat, fish and pasta dinner entrees, champagne Sunday brunch.

Grand Pizza Company, 717 Grand Ave.; call 970-627-8390. Prices $ to $$. Pizza, lunch and dinner, submarine sandwiches, cappuccino, espresso.

Lariat Saloon, 1121 Grand Ave.; call 970-627-9965. Prices $. Sandwiches, burgers, full bar.

Mountain Inn, 612 Grand Ave.; call 970-627-3385. Prices $ to $$. Mexican and American, home cooking, children's menu, full bar.

Pancho & Lefty's, 1101 Grand Ave.; call 970-627-8773. Prices $ to $$. Mexican and American dishes, full bar.

Restaurant Associations

Colorado Restaurant Association, 899 Logan St., Ste. 300, Denver, CO 80203; call 303-830-2972

Road Conditions

Colorado Dept. of Transportation / State Patrol Recordings; within a two hour drive from Denver, call 303-639-1111; statewide, call 303-639-1234.

Rocky Mountain National Park

Rocky Mountain National Park, Estes Park, CO 80517; call 970-586-1206; Kawaneeche Visitor Center 970-627-3471. For backcountry information and lost and found, call 970-586-1242.

Tourism

Colorado Statewide Information

Colorado Travel & Tourism

Authority, P.O. Box 22005, Denver, CO 80222; call 800-COLORADO; internet http://www.colorado.com.

Regional Tourism Organizations

Clear Creek County Tourism Board, P.O. Box 60, Idaho Springs, CO 80452; call 303-567-4660 or 800-88-BLAST.

Front Range Region, 2440 Pearl St., Boulder, CO 80302; call 800-444-0447 for a free Front Range Adventure Guide.

Poudre Canyon / Red Feathers Lake Tourist Council, Box 178, Red Feathers Lake, CO 80545; call 800-462-5870.

Chambers of Commerce / Visitor Bureaus

Boulder Convention & Visitors Bureau, 2440 Pearl St., Boulder, CO 80302; call 303-442-2911 or 800-444-0447.

Estes Park Area Chamber, P.O. Box 3050, Estes Park, CO 80517; call 970-586-4431 or 800-44-ESTES

Grand Lake Area Chamber, P.O. Box 57, Grand Lake, CO 80447; call 970-627-3402 or 800-531-1019.

Longmont Area Chamber, 528 N. Main St., Longmont, CO 80501; call 303-776-5295.

Loveland Chamber, 114 E. 5th St., Loveland, CO 80537; call 970-667-6311.

Lyons Chamber, P.O. Box 426, Lyons, CO 80540; call 303-823-5215.

Nederland Area Chamber, P.O. Box 85, Nederland, CO 80466; call 303-258-3936 or 800-221-0044.

Recreation

Backpacking

See Government Agencies,

Reference

Bureau of Land Management or U.S. Forest Service.
Colorado Outward Bound, 845 Pennsylvania St., Denver, CO 80203; call 303-837-0880.
Sundance Adventures, P.O. Box 1722, Boulder, CO 80306; call 303-665-5437.

Bicycling
Colorado Bicycle Adventures, P.O. Box 1301, Estes Park, CO 80517; call 970-586-4241.
Rocky Mountain Sports, 711 Grand Avenue, Grand Lake, CO 80447; call 970-627-8124.

Boating
See Government Agencies, Colorado Division of Wildlife, Colorado State Parks and U.S. Forest Service.

Climbing
Colorado Mountain School, P.O. Box 2062, Estes Park, CO 80517; call 970-586-5758.

Cross-Country Skiing / Snowshoeing
Adventures Afoot, P.O. Box 1565, Estes Park, CO 80517; call 970-586-3341.
Colorado Cross Country Ski Association, Snow Mountain Nordic Center, P.O. Box 169, Winter Park, CO 80482; call 970-887-2152.
Colorado Wilderness Sports, P.O. Box 4079, Estes Park, CO 80517; call 970-586-5648.
YMCA of the Rockies, P.O. Box 583, Association Camp, Estes Park, CO 80511; call 970-586-3341.

Fishing
See Government Agencies, Colorado Division of Wildlife, Colorado State Parks and U.S. Forest Service.
Colorado Wilderness Sports, P.O. Box 4079, Estes Park, CO

80517; call 970-586-5648.
Estes Angler, 338 West Riverside Dr., Estes Park, CO 80517; call 970-586-2110.
YMCA of the Rockies, 2515 Tunnel Road, Estes Park, CO 80517; call 970-586-3341.

Four-Wheeling
Colorado Association of Four-wheel Drive Clubs, Inc., P.O. Box 1413, Wheat Ridge, CO 80034; call 303-343-0646.

Golf
Colorado Golf Association, 5655 S. Yosemite, Ste. 101, Englewood, CO 80111; call 303-779-4653.
Colorado Golf Resort Association, 2110 Ash, Denver, CO 80222; call 303-699-GOLF.

Guides / Outfitters / Hunting
Colorado Outfitters Association, P.O. Box 1304, Parker, CO 80134; call 303-841-7760.

Hiking
Estes Mountain Guides, 1263 Giant Track, Estes Park, CO 80517; call 970-577-0712.
Step'n Up, 160 Stanley Circle, Estes Park, CO 80517; call 970-586-6109.
Walkabout Tours, 600 Moccasin Circle Dr., #3, Estes Park, CO 80517; call 970-577-9256.

Horseback Riding
Aspen Lodge and Guest Ranch, Longs Peak Route, Estes Park, CO 80517; call 970-586-8133.
Glacier Creek Stables, Rocky Mountain National Park, Estes Park, CO 80517; call 970-586-3244.
Meeker Park Lodge, Highway 7, Allenspark, CO 80517; call 303-747-2266.
Moraine Park Stables, Rocky Mountain National Park, Estes Park, CO 80517; call

970-586-2327.
National Park Village Livery, P.O. Box 2214, Estes Park, CO 80517; call 970-586-5269.
Silver Lane Stables, P.O. Box 152, Estes Park, CO 80517; call 970-586-4695.
Sombrero Ranch (Grand Lake), 3300 Airport Road, Boulder, CO 80301; call 970-627-3514.
Sombrero Ranches, Inc., 1895 Big Thompson Road, Estes Park, CO 80517; call 970-586-4577.
Wild Basin Livery, N Star Road, Allenspark, CO 80510; call 303-747-2545.
Wind River Ranch, P.O. Box 3410, Estes Park, CO 80517; call 970-586-4212.
Winding River Resort Village Campground, P.O. Box 629, Grand Lake, CO 80447; call 970-627-3215.
YMCA of the Rockies, P.O. Box 583, Association Camp, CO 80511; call 970-586-3341, ext. 1140.

Rafting
Colorado River Outfitters Association, P.O. Box 1662, Buena Vista, CO 81211; call 303-369-4632 (Denver direct).

Skiing
Colorado Ski Country USA, 160 Broadway, Ste. 1440, Denver, CO 80202; call 303-837-0793 or 303-825-7669 (snow report).

Snowmobiling
Colorado Snowmobile Association, P.O. Box 1260, Grand Lake, CO 80447; call 800-235-4480.

Tennis
Colorado Tennis Association, 1201 S. Parker Road #200, Denver, CO 80231; call 303-695-4116.

Index

Index

Photographic Credits

Dan Klinglesmith

Patrick Soran

Writer and photographer Dan Klinglesmith can trace his Colorado roots back four generations. His great-great grandparents, John and Martha Barrow, came to the "Centennial State" in 1888, settling in Crested Butte. The mining camp was too rowdy a place to raise children so they moved to Hotchkiss, homesteading a few acres outside town on what is still called Barrow Mesa. Born on the Western Slope at Grand Junction, Dan fondly remembers summers spent horseback riding amidst the buttes and valleys that were first settled by his family.

Growing up on the state's Front Range gave Dan a taste of big-city life, and he still calls Denver home. For the last decade, however, the world has become his backyard. Working as a freelance travel writer and photographer, Dan has crisscrossed the globe, penning articles for a wide variety of magazines and newspapers.

Nevertheless, he admits there's no place like home. "Colorado has it all," contends Dan. "It's a state marked with incredible natural beauty, fascinating history and diversions to occupy a lifetime." He adds, "there's no greater joy than writing about the place you love."

Raised and educated in Denver's Capitol Hill, Patrick Soran lives in the very home in which he was born. The house was purchased by his grandparents in 1936 and has served as hearth and home to three generations. Needless to say, Patrick is an enthusiastic advocate of Denver; he loves to pedal its bicycle paths, chat with friends in its urbane coffee shops, walk its tree-lined avenues and, of course, spend autumn Sundays cheering (and crying!) for the Denver Broncos.

Trained as an architect, Patrick designed luxury homes and hotel interiors for 15 years before trading T-square and triangle for computer and camera in 1990. Now he explores the world writing articles about travel, design and personalities for newspapers and magazines across the country.

Patrick is immensely proud to write about his home state. He believes Colorado has terrific wilderness and wildlife experiences, edge-of-the-envelope recreation and exciting cultural and lifestyle opportunities.